THE ESSENTIAL CLARENCE SKINNER

Clarence R. Skinner
1881-1949

THE ESSENTIAL CLARENCE SKINNER

A Brief Introduction to His Life and Writings

CHARLES HOWE, EDITOR

SKINNER HOUSE BOOKS
BOSTON

Printed in the United States.

Frontispiece portrait of Clarence R. Skinner by Joseph B. Cahill, 1948.

Text and cover design by Suzanne Morgan.

FISBN 1-55896-481-9

Library of Congress Cataloging-in-Publication Data

The essential Clarence Skinner : a brief introduction to his life and writings / Charles Howe, editor.

    p. cm.
  Includes bibliographical references.
  ISBN 1-55896-481-9 (alk. paper)
  1. Skinner, Clarence Russell, 1881-1949. 2. Universalism. I. Skinner, Clarence Russell, 1881-1949. II. Howe, Charles A., 1922-
BX9969.S55E88 2005
289.1'092--dc22

2004019616

10 9 8 7 6 5 4 3 2 1
07 06 05 04

The biographical article by Charles Howe is a shortened version of one that appeared earlier in *Clarence R. Skinner: Prophet of a New Universalism*, which is no longer in print. Material from "Worship and a Well Ordered Life" by Clarence Skinner, published in 1955 by the Universalist Historical Society and Meeting House Press, has been reprinted here by permission of Clarise L. Patton.

CONTENTS

PREFACE

CLARENCE SKINNER (1881-1949) has been widely regarded as the most important American Universalist of the twentieth century. He served on the faculty of the Crane Theological School at Tufts University for thirty-one years, the last twelve as dean, inspiring a new generation of ministers to work for the revitalization of their denomination. He was also an ecclesiastical innovator, organizing the progressive Community Church of Boston and serving as its leader for sixteen years. And Skinner was the author of more than 180 articles and addresses, as well as five books. His first book, *The Social Implications of Universalism*, published in 1915, and his *A Religion for Greatness*, published thirty years later, both had a huge impact on his denomination. As a lifelong social activist, Skinner was a leader in developing a program for Universalist social witness as America was entering the First World War. He persevered in his witness even when he was ostracized by the Tufts president and much of the faculty and denounced by the civil authorities for his pacifist position. Altogether, Skinner's influence was a major factor in the renewal of the Universalist Church, building the groundwork for its consolidation with the American Unitarian Association twelve years after his death.

Despite his many accomplishments, Clarence Skinner's life and thought are relatively unknown today. This book is designed to introduce him to today's reader and, in the process, to rescue him from the twin dangers of being forgotten and being honored in ignorance. To achieve this, a short biographical essay, an address written on the occasion of Skinner's retirement, and selections from his writings are offered here. Skinner was a prolific writer and his writings fall into a variety of categories—not only theology, philosophy, and ecclesiology but also poetry and straightforward reporting. Excerpts are presented chronologically to illustrate the evolution of his interests and thought.

CHRONOLOGY

1881	Clarence Skinner was born on March 23rd in Brooklyn, New York
1900-1904	Studied at St. Lawrence University in Canton, New York, graduating with a Bachelor of Arts degree
1904-1906	Worked as assistant to Frank Oliver Hall, minister of the Church of the Divine Paternity in New York City
1906	Ordained to the Universalist ministry
1906-1911	Served as minister of the Universalist Church in Mount Vernon, New York
1910-1919	Held office as the secretary of the Commission on Social Service for the Universalist General Convention
1911-1914	Served as minister of the Grace Universalist Church in Lowell, Massachusetts

1914-1933	Taught Applied Christianity at Crane Theological School, Tufts University, in Medford, Massachusetts
1915	Published *The Social Implications of Universalism*
1917-1919	Served as part-time minister to the Medford Hillside Universalist Church
1920-1936	Led the Community Church of Boston, of which he was a cofounder
1931-1941	Acted as contributing editor of the Unitarian periodical *Unity*
1933-1945	Served as dean of Tufts School of Religion, Crane Theological School
1937	Published *Liberalism Faces the Future*
1939	Published *Human Nature and the Nature of Evil*
1945	Published *A Religion for Greatness*
1949	Died at his summer home in Long Ridge, Connecticut
1955	Published *Worship and a Well Ordered Life*, completed not long before his death
1959	Clarence R. Skinner Award established

1963 The Unitarian Universalist Association dedicated Skinner House, a property located on Mt. Vernon Place near UUA headquarters in Boston.

1976 The Unitarian Universalist Association adopted the name Skinner House Books for its publishing imprint.

The Life of a UU Prophet

Clarence Russell Skinner, widely recognized as the foremost American Universalist of the first half of the twentieth century, was born in Brooklyn, New York, on March 23, 1881, the son of Charles Montgomery Skinner and Ada Blanchard Skinner, members of the local Universalist church. His father, a newspaper editor long associated with the *Brooklyn Eagle*, was an individualist with broad and deep interests. A prolific writer, Charles Skinner was the author of nine books and three plays in addition to his numerous newspaper articles. Taken together, his writings reflect both a love of nature and a progressive social idealism. His influence on his son was enduring and great, but the influence of young Clarence's mother is difficult to judge. Clarence Skinner remembered her as a loving woman who worked hard to maintain a dependable home environment in their Brooklyn apartment.

The couple had three sons, Clarence, Harold, and Lindley. Lindley died quite young. Clarence's uncle

Otis Augustus Skinner and cousin Cornelia Otis were two of the country's best-known actors, and Clarence seriously considered acting as a career, the path his brother Harold took.

Clarence attended public schools in Brooklyn until his difficulty with high-school mathematics prompted his father to transfer him to Erasmus Hall, one of the leading preparatory schools in the area. Erasmus's principal, Walter B. Gunnison, was a progressive educator who ran the school like a small college, an environment in which young Clarence blossomed. It was there that he met Louis Pink, who was to become a lifelong friend. In 1900, they enrolled together in the freshman class of St. Lawrence University in Canton, New York.

Walter Gunnison's brother Almon had been named president of St. Lawrence the previous year, after a successful pastorate at the Skinner family's home church in Brooklyn. The university, which was established by Universalists in 1856, included both a nonsectarian liberal arts college and a small denominational theological school. Clarence's grandfather, Charles A. Skinner, had been a Universalist minister, as had his great-grandfather, Warren Skinner, and his great-uncle, Otis A. Skinner. So young Clarence had been steeped in Universalism well before his arrival at St. Lawrence.

Skinner's college years were a time of growth. He continued his interests in dramatics and journalism, in time becoming president of the drama society and editor of the school newspaper. He was a good student, developing an especially keen interest in physics and foreign languages. In his senior year, Clarence took over the teaching responsibilities of an ill German professor. In addition, he was elected as class president and to membership in Phi Beta Kappa.

But the most dramatic event of Skinner's senior year was his engagement to Clara Louise Ayres, a classmate and fellow member of Phi Beta Kappa. Ayres was even a better student than Skinner, coming in second in the graduating class of forty, while he ranked fourth. The two seem to have been drawn to each other by their similar personalities; both were shy, studious, serious, and smart. The daughter of a wealthy family from Stamford, Connecticut, Ayres had led a sheltered life. Her parents initially opposed the engagement but relented after they met Skinner.

The fall after graduation, Skinner became assistant to Frank Oliver Hall, minister of the Church of the Divine Paternity (now known as the Fourth Universalist Society) on Central Park West in Manhattan, one of the largest and most prestigious churches in the denomination. Given his academic background, it was a surprising move, for Skinner's interest in theology and the ministry had seemed marginal.

Hall took Skinner's title as *assistant* quite literally. He assigned Skinner responsibilities as youth leader, executive secretary, and general errand boy. On one occasion, Hall ordered Skinner to go out and buy his daughter's Christmas present. Skinner got a chance for more interesting work when Hall was ill, filling the minister's pulpit for an entire month. *The Brooklyn Eagle* gave his sermons good reviews and predicted a promising future for the fledgling preacher.

On April 8, 1906, Clarence Russell Skinner was ordained to the Christian ministry at the Church of the Divine Paternity. Hall preached the ordination sermon. That summer the new Reverend Skinner accepted a call from the Universalist Church in Mount Vernon, just north of New York City. It was a small church, typical of those in which new ministers were usually settled, with a congregation of about three dozen families. The building was dilapidated, but the salary of $66 a month was considered good for an inexperienced minister. Moreover, Ayres's parents were pleased that she would be staying close to home. The two were married in Stamford on October 16, with Hall officiating before a small family gathering. After a honeymoon in Washington, D.C., the newly-weds moved into an apartment in Mount Vernon. They were seldom apart for the next forty-three years. For Clara, the adjustment to a new life was difficult, but in time she was able to find a satisfying role for herself as a minister's wife. The couple never had children, and though they sometimes considered adoption, they always postponed it to a quieter time that never came.

The five years in Mount Vernon were busy ones for Skinner. He threw himself into his ministerial tasks, maintaining a rigorous, self-imposed schedule that included a weekly quota of parish calls. Despite his basic shyness, he considered these calls an essential part of his ministry. All the administrative work of the parish fell on Skinner's shoulders as well, and the skills he had developed during his two years at Divine Paternity stood him in good stead. Skinner's early sermons were overly idealistic and cluttered with long words, but he was a gifted preacher and his idealism was soon tempered by worldly realities. Skinner's wife, who was determined that Skinner's parishioners would understand his sermons, used her considerable influence to cut down his excessively elaborate vocabulary. The hard work paid off: Church membership more than doubled, as did enrollment in the church school. It was not long before Skinner's work was attracting attention within the denomination.

Perhaps the major achievement of Skinner's tenure at Mount Vernon church was the construction of a new church building. Early in his ministry there, Skinner had invited his uncle Otis to speak at a Sunday service. Otis Skinner's fame as an actor attracted an overflow congregation, and the old building creaked and groaned so badly under the weight that the young minister feared it might collapse. Convincing the small congregation that it needed a new building and raising the necessary funds was a major undertaking, but the effort succeeded. The new church was dedicated on Easter Sunday 1910, with a full congregation on hand. Mrs. Andrew Carnegie, a member of Divine Paternity, had taken an interest in the project, and helped to raise money for a new organ by matching each contribution.

That same year, Clarence Skinner completed the requirements for a master of arts degree from St. Lawrence by taking course work at Columbia University. At about this same time, he became a pacifist. He was never to retreat from this position, even though it later brought him under strong attack.

During his two years at Divine Paternity, Skinner had often taken part in the activities of the University Settlement House on the East Side. After he moved to Mount Vernon, he made weekly trips to the city to continue his involvement. Skinner's experience at University Settlement House convinced him that while settlement houses were valuable, their overall long-term impact was marginal and an approach designed to address the root causes of social problems was necessary. American Baptist minister Walter Rauschenbusch's *Christianity and the Social Crisis* had appeared in 1907, and the Social Gospel movement in American churches was well under way. It didn't take long for Skinner to accept and expand its ideas. His mentor, Frank Oliver Hall, had made a powerful speech in 1909 at the Universalist General Convention, urging churches to accept responsibility for addressing the social problems of the day. As a result, a denominational Commission on Social Service was established, with Hall as its chair. Skinner was appointed as the Commission's secretary, probably on Hall's recommendation, and served in that capacity for a decade, making a major contribution to its work.

In the spring of 1911 Skinner accepted an invitation to candidate for the ministry of Grace Universalist

Church in Lowell, Massachusetts, a church considerably stronger and with greater opportunities for community service than the church at Mount Vernon. Early that summer Grace Church extended a call and he accepted. It was, Skinner had decided, time to move on. The Skinners moved their furniture out of their apartment, stored it in Stamford, and enjoyed a well-earned vacation before moving on to a new church, a new city, and a new challenge.

Grace Church had a constituency of some145 families. It was located in the downtown area of a rapidly growing city, one of two thriving Universalist churches in Lowell. As reported in the *Universalist Leader*, the church year got off to a promising start:

> The pastor, Rev. Clarence R. Skinner, is giving a series of sermons Sunday mornings on "The New Religion." The series consists of seven sermons running from October 8th to November 19th inclusive, in which as many aspects of the important subject will be treated. Beginning last Sunday evening, with an address by Dr. Perkins of Lynn, a series of evening services will be continued regularly for some weeks. At these meetings vital questions now confronting the American people will be discussed.

The evening series, named the Lowell Forum, was an immediate success. Skinner, doubtless remembering what a draw his uncle Otis had been in Mount Vernon, worked hard to schedule as many well-known speakers as possible. On most occasions the church, which seated between four hundred and five hundred people, was full. The program consisted of a short worship service, a collection to help cover expenses, and an address by the evening's speaker, followed by discussion. The forum provided a model of how a church might become an effective agent for change without sacrificing its traditional function of worship.

It is evident from the record that the church was growing substantially at this time. By the end of 1914 there were some 260 families in the church. Skinner was a conscientious pastor, and as his counseling load and parish calling increased, he developed the habit of working late at night. It was a demanding life, but Skinner appears to have thrived on it. Meanwhile, his reputation within the denomination was increasing rapidly.

One of those invited to speak at the forum during the 1913-1914 church year was Lee S. McCollester, dean of the Crane Theological School at Tufts. The Skinners had invited McCollester to supper before the evening's program, and during the course of the meal, the dean said to his host, "I'd like to have you come down to Tufts." Skinner didn't take the remark seriously, but not long afterward he received an offer to join the Crane faculty as professor of Applied Christianity. Although he had been at Lowell for only three years, it did not take him long to decide. He had found that he loved to teach, and the prospect of making it a career while still serving the church was too tempting to refuse. Thus in the fall of 1914 Clarence Skinner, a thirty-three-year-old with no theological degree and but eight years of parish experience, entered the academic world. His ministry at Lowell had proved a stepping-stone to greater things, and Grace Church was proud of him. As his successor, Herbert Benton, later put it, "Skinner had a great success there. All the church was loud in praise."

When Lee McCollester came to the Crane Theological School in 1912, the school was at its lowest ebb, with four full-time students. In fact, it was only through *Universalist Leader* editor Frederick Bisbee's concerted effort to muster support for the school that prevented the Tufts College administration from closing it down. McCollester had finally been persuaded to accept the deanship after his demands were met for an adequate salary and the guarantee of a free hand in rebuilding the school's program. Under his leadership the faculty was strengthened and the school began to show steady growth. Herman Bumpus had just assumed the college presidency when Skinner arrived in the fall of 1914. At that time the student body numbered 479, with thirteen students in the theological school. The new professor was given a heavy teaching load from the start—over the first two years he was listed as teaching eighteen courses in Applied Christianity, History of Religions, Church History, and Religious Education. Skinner lost no time in organizing the Department of Applied Christianity, and by the 1916-1917 school year, the department offered courses in social psychology, principles and methods of social service, home and foreign missions, country church problems, and laboratory social work, the latter requiring students to work in approved social agencies, settlement houses, or charitable organizations.

Despite this seemingly overwhelming teaching and administrative load, Skinner found time to write. In 1915 his first book, *The Social Implications of Universalism*, appeared and had an immediate impact on the denomination. Its foreword began with the statement, "How to transform this old earth into the Kingdom of Heaven—that's the primal question." The book spelled out the implications of Universalism for the Social Gospel in sweeping terms, going well beyond the scope of Protestant Christianity. Following the foreword were eleven short chapters: "The Challenge," "A Free Church," "God and Democracy," "The Nature of Man," "Brotherhood," "Social Motive," "The Leadership of Jesus," "Hell and Salvation," "The New Unity," "The Final Triumph," and "The Larger Faith." These had also appeared in serial form in the *Universalist Leader*.

To the present-day reader, Skinner's views in this book may seem naive, his optimism unjustified. Moreover, he failed to address adequately some important questions, among them the relationship of Christianity to the "larger faith," the question of an afterlife, and the nature of individual salvation in the interim period before the "final triumph." It was, of course, written at a time when the proponents of the Social Gospel were filled with hope, an optimism that would soon be tempered if not destroyed by the onset of world war. Nevertheless, *The Social Implications of Universalism* represents a serious attempt to spell out a prophetic and comprehensive theological, ecclesiastical, and social program for the denomination, the first such effort in many years. As such, this work established Clarence Skinner as one of Universalism's leading spokesmen. From today's perspective, it can be seen as a turning point for the denomination and Skinner as the herald of the new Universalism to come.

That fall the Commission on Social Service submitted its Declaration of Social Principles to the Universalist General Convention. The Declaration, adopted as the denomination's basis for social witness, clearly shows Skinner's influence as the Commission's secretary. The preamble to the Declaration's working program states, "Through all the agencies of the church we shall endeavor to educate and inspire the community and the nation to a keener social consciousness and a truer vision of the kingdom of God on the earth." It goes on to advocate the strengthening of marriage and the nurturing of children, a more equitable economic system, the rights of women, free and open discussion as "the soul of democracy," prohibition of the manufacture and sale of alcoholic beverages, the institution of "some form of social insurance," and formation of a world federation to secure peace. In conclusion, the Declaration outlines a program for "completing humanity":

First: An Economic Order which shall give to every human being an equal share in the common gifts of God, and in addition all that he shall earn by his own labor.

Second: A Social Order in which there shall be equal rights for all, special privileges for none, the help of the strong for the weak until the weak become strong.

Third: A Moral Order in which all human law and action shall be an expression of the moral order of the universe.

Fourth: A Spiritual Order which shall build out of the growing lives of living men the growing temple of the living God.

Despite his writing and his denominational involvement, Skinner's primary commitment throughout these years was to his teaching and his students at Crane. "I know of no way to accomplish [the restructuring of] the social order except through education," he told the Sunday School Convention in 1917. He developed three rules for successful teaching: First, a teacher must love to teach; second, a teacher must inspire, not just communicate information and ideas; and third, a teacher must always be a student. It was evident to those who knew Skinner in the classroom that he qualified easily on the first of these requirements. The second he fulfilled not only by virtue of his teaching style but also through close personal contact with his students at school and at his home. And Skinner was in fact a student his entire life, continuously reflecting on his own life experiences and reading voraciously.

The same year that Skinner spoke to the Sunday School Convention, the United States entered the World War, and his pacifism soon became controversial. He was one of only a handful of Universalist ministers to publicly declare a pacifist position. The overwhelming majority of his colleagues were active supporters of the war effort, as were the administration and faculty of Tufts College. The military took over most of the facilities of the theological school, and the few students who remained in the school attended most of their classes in the dean's living room. After the Boston newspapers identified Skinner as a pacifist, he was publicly ostracized; President Bumpus became so angry with him that he refused to acknowledge him when they met on campus. Most of the faculty, frustrated at their inability to change Skinner's mind, even through prayer at faculty meetings, shunned him as well and many called for his dismissal. An atmosphere of near hysteria prevailed on campus; Bumpus had even provided Indian clubs for the students so that they could repel any enemy attack on College Hill.

Fortunately Skinner had several supporters in the faculty, including McCollester, who defended the young professor's right to hold and express his own views, even though McCollester was not a pacifist himself. Once, when Skinner was speaking in Concord, people threw rotten eggs at him, but he never wavered, nor did he completely lose his sense of humor. In a letter to Bumpus in July 1917, Skinner wrote:

> I hope that among the great cares you can find some relaxation and rest this summer, and that college matters will so shape themselves that you may be relieved of some of the great anxieties of the past. I doubt not that I have been one of these causes of worry.
> Sincerely,
> your pacifist friend,
> Clarence R. Skinner

Despite this attempt at lightheartedness, the treatment he received during the war hurt Skinner deeply, and the wounds never completely healed.

The end of the war brought a renewal of the nation's former optimism. As President Harding put it, "America's present need is not heroics but healing, not nostrums but normalcy." Skinner shared this view. He wrote a piece in January 1919 titled "The World Soul," which eloquently described what Skinner saw as the dawning of a new day of peace and fulfillment throughout a united world. Skinner's optimism was short-lived, however. The world was not ready to hear his message. After Skinner spoke in Meriden, Connecticut, in February 1919, the local paper quoted the city's mayor as saying he was "more than disgusted at the reported reference to Lenin in the so-called lecture. . . . We want no more of that stuff put out here and this may as well be known now as later, and trouble prevented." To make matters worse, Skinner's part-time ministry at the Medford Hillside Universalist Church, adjacent to the Tufts campus, was terminated at the end of that year. Although he had managed a successful church program for the past two years and made the church a working laboratory, with students participating in the church school and occasionally preaching, mounting criticism of Skinner's pacifist position forced him to resign.

Skinner was undeterred. He delivered an address to the American Forum at Faneuil Hall on December 21 that prompted complaints to the local district attorney, Nathan A. Tufts, who in turn wrote the Tufts administration, asking for an investigation of Skinner. Fortunately, Bumpus had been replaced as college president by John Cousens, who replied to the district attorney,

> I have received some report of the meeting, from which it appears that after Professor Skinner's speech had been delivered there was some little excitement and disturbance in connection with the speeches from the floor. I fail to understand why a disturbance should have resulted from anything which Professor Skinner said.
>
> I have a very high regard for Professor Skinner personally as I know him to be a man of sincerity and honesty of purpose.

District Attorney Tufts answered promptly:

> I have a letter before me from two persons who heard his speech at Faneuil Hall, and they say that he approved the action taken by the I.W.W.s [members of the International Workers of the World, a labor union outlawed in 1917] at Centralia when four soldiers were shot during a parade; that he called the members of the American Legion "anarchists"; that he spoke against the measure introduced by Representative Johnson of Washington designed to curb undesirable immigration.

President Cousens informed Tufts that he had read the speech and did not interpret it the same way, again reaffirming his confidence in Skinner, and the matter was dropped.

That same month, Cousens received a letter from an alumnus, enclosing a clipping from a Lynn newspaper that referred to Skinner's address, "Industrial Democracy," at the Congregational church. Skinner had called for improved working conditions and the right to collective bargaining. "In view of the present campaign to raise money for increasing salaries of Tufts professors," wrote the alumnus, "I should like to inquire if this is the kind of 'stuff' which we are expected to support." It was the second time in a few weeks that Skinner's views had been referred to as "stuff." Cousens was understandably diplomatic in his reply. He wrote, "I think you will recognize in the account . . . some of the usual American newspaper extravagance of statement," and he further suggested that the alumnus make allowances for an honest difference of opinion.

Skinner's liberal views evoked suspicion not only in America but abroad as well. When he applied in 1922 for a year's leave of absence to visit India under the auspices of those "interested in international and industrial peace," the British government rejected his visa application, probably afraid that his visit would prove disruptive.

Not surprisingly, Skinner became discouraged by the many criticisms leveled against him, some of it from within his own denomination. The United States was in a state of reaction to liberal idealism; its membership in the League of Nations had been rejected; the Universalist denomination was experiencing an alarming decline, with few churches committed to implementing its social program, and the Social Gospel movement was all but dead. Out of his deep disappointment, but still with ultimate hope, Skinner wrote "In Times of Disillusion," published in *Unity* on April 24, 1924. It begins on a pessimistic note: "The world has grown unutterably old—A place of bitter disillusionment." But by the end Skinner is buoyant, almost defiant: "I'll still proclaim the 'Vision Splendid,' Till it strikes God-fire in old and broken hearts. . . . God's unsurrendered! SO AM I! . . . I light the candle and—I DREAM."

This piece represents Clarence Skinner at his poetic best and gives insight into the prophetic vision that was central to his being, the transformation of "this old earth" into "the Kingdom of Heaven." The change might take longer than Skinner had once thought, but he continued to have faith that it would happen someday. In the meantime, he intended to do all he could to help that transformation along and to keep that vision alive. In a time when many surrendered, he was indeed "unsurrendered."

Fortunately Skinner was soon to find a new project that would help lift him out of his disillusionment and disappointment. In the fall of 1919, during the time he was being forced out of his ministry to the Medford Hillside congregation, he conceived a plan for a radically new kind of church, one that would be all-inclusive, unrestrained by any denominational ties. It marked a disengagement from the mainstream of the Universalist denomination that would continue for the next fifteen years. Ever conscientious, Skinner took pains to keep President Cousens informed about what he was doing, and Cousens only asked Skinner to do nothing that would embarrass Dean McCollester.

In October Skinner circulated a flyer advertising a meeting to discuss the possible organization of a community church in Boston. John Haynes Holmes, who had just severed his Unitarian ties and led the transformation of the Unitarian Church of the Messiah into the independent Community Church of New York, came to the meeting. He and Skinner had been drawn together by their theological and social liberalism, pacifism, and shared desire to create a model for a more relevant church. Although few attended the meeting, there appeared to be enough interest in the proposal to proceed. Accordingly, Skinner began a series of experimental services with Holmes scheduled as the first speaker. On January 11 a congregation of three hundred assembled in Steinert Hall on Boylston Street to hear his address, "The Character and Meaning of the Community Church Movement." Skinner himself preached on the following Sunday, followed by such notables as Bishop Paul Jones, Norman Thomas, and Frank Oliver Hall. Skinner's experience with the Lowell Forum undoubtedly played a part in the planning. Attendance during those early services ranged from sixty to five hundred, with Holmes attracting the largest crowds.

On the basis of this encouraging start, an organizational meeting of "The Community Church of Boston" was held on October 31, 1920, following the Sunday service. The new church elected several officers, including Skinner as chairman, and adopted a Statement of Purpose. After revision and approval by the church's constituency, the Statement read,

> The Community Church of Boston is a free fellowship of men and women united for the study of universal religion, seeking to apply ethical ideals to individual life and the co-operative principle to all forms of social and economic life.

The only condition for membership was subscription to the following Bond of Union:

> We, the undersigned, accepting the stated Purpose of this Church, so join ourselves together that we may help one another, may multiply the power of each through mutual fellowship, and thereby promote most effectively the cause of truth, righteousness and love in the world.

For the next fifteen years, Clarence Skinner filled two full-time jobs—member of the faculty at Crane Theological School and leader of the Community Church of Boston (the traditional term *minister* was not used). He did much of the church's administrative and pastoral work, attended all meetings, planned and led the Sunday services, presided over rites of passage, and preached about three times a year. After the church became established, Skinner was voted a modest salary, which helped offset some of his personal expenses as leader. The services reflected the "rational worship" to which the congregation was committed and were simple in format: an invocation stating the church's purpose and creating an atmosphere for worship, three hymns (often with new words), a reading, a nonpetitionary prayer, and the sermon. A forum consisting of comments, discussion, and questions and answers followed each service. Holmes preached monthly, asking only that his expenses be covered. Other speakers were chosen carefully and included such well-known men and women as Rabbi Stephen S. Wise, Bertrand Russell,

H. V. Kaltenborn, Maude Royden, Will Durant, Reinhold Niebuhr, Sarujini Naidu, Sherwood Eddy, William Ernest Hocking, Kirtley Mather, John Dietrich, and Margaret Sanger. A collection of addresses delivered at the church was published in 1931 under the title *A Free Pulpit in Action.*

Services were held in rented halls throughout the period of Skinner's leadership, with the average attendance rising from 175 in 1921 to about 1,200 by 1926. The church's involvement in the Sacco and Vanzetti case (the Skinners attended many sessions of the trial), the Scottsboro case, aid to the Republican government of Spain, and advocacy of Margaret Sanger's right to speak in Boston were perhaps the most publicized examples of its social concern. Skinner regarded his involvement in the Community Church as "a thrilling experience."

Meanwhile, the Crane Theological School began to recover from its outrage over Skinner's pacifist position after the war ended. Skinner organized his Department of Applied Christianity into one of the best of its kind for that day. His course in social ethics, "a study of the great ethical concepts of Jesus as applied to modern society," was particularly popular. It focused on various reform movements and students tried to construct a picture of what a Christianized society would look like. Another popular course dealing directly with social work consisted of one lecture or conference per week, with students spending the rest of their time on fieldwork with approved Boston agencies.

"This experience in the laboratory of humanity," the catalog read, "is of inestimable value to all who are to deal with problems of leadership in industry, schools, communities and churches."

With the student body growing, Skinner's heavy teaching load was lightened somewhat by two additions to the school's faculty: J. A. C. Fagginer Auer in 1924 as professor of church history and philosophy of religion and John Ratcliff in 1927 as professor of religious education. Skinner's old mentor, Frank Oliver Hall, had joined the faculty in 1919 as professor of homiletics and continued in that position for ten years. He was replaced by Alfred S. Cole. Bruce Brotherston joined the faculty in 1930 to teach philosophy in both the theological school and the college. McCollester himself served not only as dean, but also as professor of religious literature and college chaplain.

In 1929 Skinner was appointed as vice dean to relieve the aging McCollester from some of his duties. Teaching remained his top priority, however, and his willingness to express his own convictions in the classroom, while stimulating to all and inspiring to many, on occasion proved disturbing. During his criticism of the verdict in the Sacco-Vanzetti case, one student became so angry that he picked up his books and walked out of the classroom. Another student left school and abandoned his plans to enter the ministry in reaction to Skinner's views.

Throughout this period, Skinner continued to write extensively. Between 1921 and 1932, a total of fifty-six articles appeared under his name, several of them long enough to appear in serial form. His articles began to appear in *Unity*, a historically Unitarian periodical of which John Haynes Holmes was the editor. Skinner eventually became a contributing editor. Skinner's previous articles were primarily restricted to the denominational magazine the *Universalist Leader*, renamed the *Christian Leader* in 1926. This change may have been prompted by Skinner's sense of alienation from his own denomination, but it was more likely an outcome of his involvement with the Community Church and expanding religious horizons.

At any rate, unlike John Haynes Holmes, Skinner retained his denominational connection. The humanist-theist debate was at its height during this period, and while Skinner warmly welcomed humanists to the Community Church's pulpit, he felt strongly that the church should not restrict itself by embracing humanism as its guiding philosophy. "Any church that is as broad as the community must surely be glad to enfold humanism," he said, "and any true humanism . . . must be willing to co-operate with a church which takes the whole community as its field, and the help of all people as its high goal."

On October 27, 1932, McCollester, by then seventy-three years old, resigned as dean of the school, the name of which changed in 1925 to Tufts School of Religion, Crane Theological School, to reflect its closer connection with the college and attract a broader student body. The school had grown significantly during McCollester's twenty-year tenure: The physical plant had been expanded and improved and the student body had grown from four to forty-five, including a number of Unitarians and other non-Universalists. In his letter of resignation to the Board of Trustees, McCollester wrote, "It is of course not for me to dictate as to my successor, but it is proper for me to express to you the wish that the new Dean shall be Dr. Skinner." The trustees agreed. Skinner took over his new duties at once and was officially installed at a college worship service the following February. Even before his installation he made it clear that changes could be expected under his leadership. In addressing the Universalist ministers of the Boston area on "The Universalist Church Twenty-five Years Hence," he predicted (accurately) that the denomination would become divided into conservative and progressive wings and that he would promote the latter.

Taking up his new responsibilities with characteristic enthusiasm, Skinner lost no time in becoming a strong advocate for his students, protecting them from unfair criticism and creating a dean's loan fund for those who were needy. The Skinners moved from Cambridge to a home on the Tufts campus to be nearer the students and Clarence's work.

Despite his new administrative responsibilities, Skinner remained first and foremost a master teacher who continued to command his students' respect by his careful preparation, depth of knowledge, communication skills, and concern for them as individuals. There was, however, a certain standoffishness about him, undoubtedly stemming from his shyness. Whereas students might have referred to his predecessor as "Mac," to them he was always "Dean Skinner" or "Dr. Skinner." Former students have recalled how this shyness often made Skinner's contacts with them outside the classroom awkward, as when, out of a sense of responsibility as dean, he visited them in their dormitory rooms or had them to his home for dinner. Conversations were strained as he tried hard to be sociable and friendly. In the classroom, however, Skinner was a different person—stimulating, confident, engaged, his teaching regularly enlivened by spontaneous wit. When a student wrote on an exam paper, "Nirvana means nothing to me," Skinner gave him full credit and commented, "I am glad you have reached that state." In addition to his administrative responsibilities as dean, he usually taught two courses each semester. His courses in comparative religions and social ethics were especially popular.

Meanwhile, Skinner's theological views, once considered radical, had gained wide acceptance within the denomination, even if many of his social views had not. The Washington Avowal of Faith, adopted unanimously by the Universalist General Convention in 1935, clearly reflected Skinner's theology, and Robert Cummins, a theological liberal like Skinner, was appointed as the Universalists' general superintendent, the denomination's highest position, in 1938.

In 1936 Skinner resigned his position as leader of the Community Church of Boston. His increased responsibilities at Crane were undoubtedly a factor, but he also felt that after fifteen years the church would profit by new, full-time leadership. Unlike the Mount Vernon church, which did not long survive the end of Skinner's successful ministry, the Community Church continues to this day as a member of the Unitarian Universalist Association. John Haynes Holmes, reflecting on Skinner's "thirty years and more" of "work and happiness" with the church, recalled that "in storms of bitterness more terrible in World War II than any hurricane of wrath known as World War I, this Boston church stood like a lighthouse at black midnight, shedding afar its saving light to guide good ships."

With his promotion to the deanship and his resignation from church leadership, Clarence Skinner entered a new phase of his life. Thereafter he focused his energies almost exclusively on education, through his classroom teaching, many speaking engagements, and extensive writings. Over the next decade he wrote four books plus some sixty articles, most of the latter published in the *Christian Leader* rather than in *Unity*, signaling his return to Universalism's mainstream. In his Phi Beta Kappa address delivered at Tufts in 1934, entitled "This Revolutionary Age," Skinner called on scholars to recognize and address the social revolution that was going on all around them. Certainly his credentials for giving such an address had been firmly established in academic circles. He had been awarded honorary doctorates from Meadville Theological School in 1926 and St.

Lawrence University in 1933 and had been considered for the presidency of St. Lawrence before he withdrew his name.

In 1937 Skinner published his second book, *Liberalism Faces the Future*, in which he defined *liberalism* as "the system that opposed illiberalism" rather than a body of knowledge, claiming it to be undefinable in static terms: "It can never be inherited, but must always be won by a new battle for each generation." Two years later *Human Nature and the Nature of Evil* appeared, in which Skinner first reviewed the approaches to the problem proposed by Barthianism, nihilism, Christian Science, Freudianism, and environmentalism, all of which he found wanting. He then addressed the subject from the standpoint of liberalism, claiming that although evil appears to be "an integral part of the normal man," the liberal also recognizes man's good nature and finds evil a stimulus to search for what is better. On the other hand, he argued, it is abnormal for good to produce evil. "There are not many," he wrote, "who would want sickness because they are well." There is in life a creative power that works toward unity; progress toward this unity is the answer to evil. In both these books, Skinner's old concern for social improvement comes through clearly.

Meanwhile, the Crane Theological School had grown steadily under Skinner's leadership. By 1938 there were fifty-four students and a faculty of thirteen, most of them part-time but with a broad range of talents and interests. The composition of the student body was

27

also quite varied, it being an article of faith with Skinner to make the school as inclusive as possible: Universalists, Unitarians, Congregationalists, Episcopalians, and Greek Orthodox of diverse backgrounds and varying abilities were all part of the mix.

The years during World War II were difficult for Skinner. He had entered his sixties, his energy was beginning to wane, and he had no opportunity to rest from his work. While his own pacifism never became a subject of controversy, he must have derived satisfaction from the strong antiwar stands taken by the Community Church and many of his students. As the war was drawing to a close in 1945, Skinner retired. He was only sixty-four, but he had undergone major surgery for cancer during the academic year, and he felt too tired to continue. Tufts honored him at commencement with a doctor of divinity degree, his third honorary degree. Despite his ill health, Skinner managed to complete another book, *A Religion for Greatness*, which was published that same year. It was dedicated to his old friend Louis Pink, who had made significant contributions to the greater good through his work in public health, housing, and insurance. The book reveals how Skinner's thinking had evolved over the years. It was to exert a significant influence in directing Universalism beyond the limits of Christianity and toward a universal religion.

Skinner had always had a mystical bent, but in *A Religion for Greatness*, it became full-blown, with his practical social emphasis enriched by a deep-seated mysticism. He called for men and women to go deeper and to recognize that a radical religion underlies all things and is indeed *the great reality* that asserts "one impressive fact—namely, man touches infinity; his home is in immensity; he lives, moves, and has his being in eternity. This magnificent assertion is man's greatest affirmation." Skinner discussed how this radical religion could be applied to economics, race issues, politics, society, and science. If applied to economics, for example, the world would no longer tolerate a difference between wealth and poverty, surplus and starvation.

Skinner was confident that out of the evolutionary process, men and women would come to a mystical insight of their place in the universe and be inspired to live together in a new way, moving toward what he termed "the unities and the universals." The *unities* are things as they truly are, interconnected in a functional whole. *Universals* represents a system of values that moves things toward what they might ideally be. The attainment of these ideals is dependent on "a system of values which stresses the largest possible *Weltanschauung*, or world outlook," with divisive "partialisms" overcome. There is a strong similarity here to the Seventh Principle, adopted by the Unitarian Universalist Association in the 1980s, which promotes "respect for the interdependent web of all existence of which we are a part." In this context the web is the ultimate unity (and also the source of other functional unities, such as planet earth, or the human family, or economic systems, or faith and social reform), while the universals are the basic values that must be operative in progress toward the ideal.

"The religion of greatness looks to the day," Skinner wrote in conclusion, "when truth, goodness and beauty will become indivisible parts of the all-embracing unity and universal." Clarence Skinner did not live to see the Kingdom of Heaven on earth, but he had faith that it would come nevertheless. The herald of a new Universalism was to remain unsurrendered to the end.

Clarence Skinner was a prolific and earnest writer, unafraid to address the pressing theological and social problems of his times. His writings, influential in their day, are important to the contemporary reader chiefly for the insight they give into the issues confronting Universalism and the changing theological and social context in which he lived. However, Skinner's students remember him best not as a writer, social activist, or ecclesiastical reformer but as an inspiring teacher. He would have derived great satisfaction from the efforts of the "Humilati," a group of his former students who worked to "universalize" Universalism along the general lines that he had advocated.

The Skinners had looked forward to the time when Clarence would retire and they would be able to enjoy travel and leisure together. They had been to Europe nine times over the years and had visited every country on the continent, but there was still much more of the world to see. Unfortunately, their plans were hampered by Skinner's illness, with their trips becoming shorter and carefully spaced. Several times he was confined to bed, often working on manuscripts while lying down. It's likely that he was working at this time on the three manuscripts that were published posthumously as *Worship and a Well Ordered Life.*

Not long after Skinner's retirement, the alumni of Crane Theological School commissioned an oil portrait of him, to be hung in Crane Chapel with those of his predecessors as dean. The sittings, which were held in the studio of the artist, Joseph B. Cahill, in Portland, Maine, proved extremely tiring for Skinner, as did the necessary travel. The portrait was unveiled in December 1948, with hundreds on hand for the ceremony. John Haynes Holmes, Skinner's friend from the Community Church experiment, was the principal speaker for the occasion.

Meanwhile the cancer continued to spread, and by the spring of 1948, doctors told Skinner that it had entered his bloodstream. He was deeply disturbed by the report, reacting with uncharacteristic emotion, and spent several days preparing instructions for the disposition of his most important possessions. He decided to leave his extensive collection of religious artifacts, accumulated during his travels, to the Crane Theological School and his books to the General Theological Library. The task had a calming effect. After it was completed, Skinner resumed work on his manuscripts.

Skinner and his wife spent the summer of 1949 at their summer home in Long Ridge, Connecticut. Louis

Pink and Alfred Cole, two of his closest friends, visited the couple there, sensing that the end was near. Pink urged Skinner to go to the hospital, but he refused. Nevertheless, Clara Skinner ordered an ambulance, hoping that he would change his mind when it arrived. He did not. When he saw the two attendants, he looked at her and said, "You know that I don't want to go the hospital." The attendants were sent away; Clarence had stubbornly won the battle. Within a week, on August 27, Clarence Skinner died at the age of sixty-eight. The funeral was held in Stamford on the 30th. Cole, Pink, John Ratcliff, Cornelius Greenway (a former student), and Roger Etz (former general superintendent of the General Convention) participated in the service. Skinner was buried at the cemetery in Long Ridge, not far from where he and his wife had spent many summer vacations. Later, memorial services were held at Tufts and at the Community Church of Boston.

Many tributes were paid to Clarence Skinner following his death, including the following resolution, written on behalf of the Tufts faculty by Cole and Ratcliff, his successor as dean:

The members of the Faculty of Arts and Sciences of Tufts College desire to express their deep sense of loss at the death of Clarence Russell Skinner at Stamford, Conn., August 27, 1949. Dr. Skinner joined our faculty in 1914 as Professor of Applied Christianity; in 1933 he became Dean of the School of Religion, retiring in 1945 after thirty-one years of service.

From the many relationships and associations with Dean Skinner, which will long be remembered by faculty and students, we can record only a few ways in which he enriched and stimulated the life of our college community.

We would especially recall:

His love for his fellow men and his constant defense of human rights and civil liberties.

His untiring effort to erase racial and class barriers.

His uncompromising support of principles he felt to be right, in the face of severe criticism and hostility.

His outstanding ability as a preacher and lecturer.

His classroom teaching and its stimulating effect on the minds of his students.

His home on Sawyer Avenue, where Mrs. Skinner and he were generous in their hospitality to students, faculty, and guests at the college.

His ability as a writer to make clear and concise the great issues of liberal religion.

His untiring efforts in the cause of peace and understanding between the nations of the world.

His great interest in the universals and unities of life calling for a religion of greatness which would transcend all creeds.

His leadership in founding the Community Church of Boston and his far-reaching influence in other liberal institutions throughout the nation.

If to these notations could be added the personal tribute of each member of the faculty, it still would be only a small indication of the outstanding service of Dean Skinner to Tufts College, and but a small measure of the sense of indebtedness of the faculty for his life and work among us.

Sources

Gaines, Charles A., "Clarence R. Skinner: Image of a Movement," unpublished. B.D. Thesis, Crane Theolo-gical School, 1961 (copy in Andover-Harvard Theological Library, Harvard Divinity School), and unpublished notes based on interviews with Clara A. Skinner (copies in Andover-Harvard Theological Library).

_____,"Clarence R. Skinner: The Dark Years," *Annual Journal of the Universalist Historical Society*, Vol. III, 1962, pp. 1-13.

John Haynes Holmes, *I Speak for Myself* (New York: Harper & Brothers, 1959), p. 227.

Howe, Charles A., ed., *Clarence R. Skinner: Prophet of a New Universalism* (Boston: Skinner House Books, 1999).

Hunt, James D., "The Liberal Theology of Clarence R. Skinner," *Journal of the Universalist Historical Society*, Vol. VII, 1967-1968, pp. 102-120.

Miller, Russell E., *The Larger Hope: The Second Century of the Universalist Church in America, 1870-1970* (Boston: Unitarian Universalist Association, 1985), pp. 493-509.

Seaburg, Alan, "The Writings of Dean Skinner: A Bibliography," *Annual Journal of the Universalist Historical Society*, Vol. V, 1964-1965, pp. 65-67.

Skinner, Clarence R., "Lowell Social Forum," *Universalist Leader*, Vol. XVIII, February 13, 1915, pp. 153-154.

———, *The Social Implications of Universalism*, reprinted in the *Annual Journal of the Universalist Historical Society*, Vol. V, 1964-1965, pp. 89-122.

———, *A Religion for Greatness* (Boston: Universalist Publishing House, 1945, reprinted 1958).

———, *Worship and a Well Ordered Life* (Boston: Universalist Historical Society and Meeting House Press, 1955).

This speech by John Haynes Holmes was prepared for a testimonial dinner for Skinner sponsored by the alumni of the Tufts College School of Religion and held in Boston on October 8, 1945. It was published in The Christian Leader, *January 19, 1946. Holmes, minister of the Community Church of New York, had worked closely with Skinner in the organization and initial work of the Community Church of Boston.*

CLARENCE R. SKINNER, OUTSTANDING RELIGIOUS LEADER IN DARK AND DIREFUL TIMES

I DEEPLY REGRET my unavoidable absence from this happy occasion held in honor of my dear friend and colleague, Clarence Skinner. I am held in New York by a sudden and quite unexpected crisis . . . .

From one point of view, it is just as well perhaps that I am not with you, for if I were present, I should have to pick a quarrel with Mr. Skinner. The most just and generous of men with other people, I must complain bitterly that he is neither just nor generous with himself. Unassuming, unpretentious, unassertive, he betrays us into undervaluing his great qualities of mind and heart. As a preacher, he is so quiet and even-tempered, that we do not always realize that we are listening to one of the great preachers of our generation. As a professor and dean of a theological school, he is as modest as a light hidden under a bushel, and thus not appreciated to his full desert as a scholar and teacher. As a man he is utterly simple and serene, and thus no advertiser of his heroic qualities.

Clarence Skinner shouts not from the housetops. He blows no trumpets in the streets. He puts on no shows, organizes no parades. He never makes a noise. Therefore do I, who have been a disturber of the silences all my life, make a loud noise for him. He has earned acclaim, applause, and celebration—and I rejoice that I am one of the goodly company who are lifting up their voices in his praise.

Clarence Skinner has been an outstanding religious leader in dark and direful times. In his thought and life and spirit, he has been unfailingly and courageously progressive—a pioneer along paths of dangerous advance. Holding fast to the eternal verities, he has led the thinking of his age to new understanding and farther vision of the truth. Remaining loyal to the church in which he was born and reared, he has yet widened the borders of his tent to embrace the concept of a universal and thus inclusive religion of mankind. Firm in the conviction that faith must minister to men's stricken souls, he has caught the vision of a faith that must serve society as well, and in a world shaken to its foundations, he has been one of the outstanding champions of a socialized Christianity.

Clear in thought and utterance, stalwart in conviction, prophetic in spirit, gallant in defense of freedom, tolerant of differing opinion, a man of peace even in time of war, a true lover of men and of their common brotherhood, Clarence Skinner's record through forty years is a thing to lift the heart . . . .

[Holmes then spoke of Skinner's part in establishing the Community Church of Boston] If, as Emerson said, "an institution is the lengthened shadow of a great man," then is the Boston Community Church the lengthened shadow of Dean Skinner.

My dear Skinner, I salute you. As these words are read, I shall be thinking of you and thus with you in spirit.

You and I have been together through many years—and they have been testing years. I search my mind in vain for any occasion when we have not been in sweet and full accord. I have always admired you as a colleague, and have come to love you as a brother. May we grow old together, that I may share your wisdom and affection to the end.

Skinner wrote the following article for the Universalist Leader *to describe the impact of the innovative social forums he introduced when he began his ministry at Lowell. The article appeared on February 13, 1915, soon after he left the church to accept a position at Tufts University.*

LOWELL SOCIAL FORUM

A FORUM has been in operation at Grace Church, Lowell, Mass., for four years. Some of the most brilliant speakers of America and England have delivered messages from this platform, and the response in this community has been hardy, attendance averaging between two hundred and four hundred. Several effects have been noted. First, the attendance of the unchurched, especially men. Second, the attendance of men and women representative of the various labor groups, such as unionists, socialists, etc. Third, the influence of these meetings beyond the narrow circle of those who attend. The press has been generous in reporting the speeches, and these speeches have been eagerly read by large numbers of the public. Fourth, it has placed the pulpit of Grace Church at the front as one of the recognized agencies of social advance in the community. Fifth, and to the mind of the writer, the most important of all, it has united the social question with religion in the minds of the people. The great need and demand of the age is for a spiritual interpretation of the whole of life. No other institution can do this more vigorously than the forum. Sixth, the immediate effect upon the church is beginning to be felt in the morning congregation. Many families, finding in the forum a satisfaction of their religious needs, have come to the regular services of the church. Seventh, the effect upon the other churches of the city is by no means to be overlooked. It has stimulated their social service activities, and some churches in other sections of the city are using similar methods.

Soon after Skinner came to Tufts University he began writing The Social Implications of Universalism. *The book was published in 1915 and had a great impact on the denomination.*

THE SOCIAL IMPLICATIONS
OF UNIVERSALISM

THE CHALLENGE

LET US MEET the issues of our time with intellectual frankness and with moral courage. Let us recognize the challenging facts of our day, and answer them with truth and with reason.

The fact is that the traditional Protestant Church is dying, dying hard with colors flying, and battling heroically, but nevertheless dying. It ought to be so. The theology on which it is built is dying; the individualism which called it into being is dying; the social order which it expressed is dying. Why should it not also die? . . .

The passing of the traditional Protestant Church does not mean that man ceases to be a religious animal; it means that he is more religious, and that he wants his religion in bigger and more vital terms. . . .

There is no danger that religion should pass out of life. There *is* danger that the Church may cease to be the voice of religion. The challenge of our day to the Christian Church is evidence of society's need of religion, but of religion in terms of contemporary life, a religion which will be founded on a twentieth century psychology and theology, a religion which is throbbing with the dynamic of democracy, a spirituality which expresses itself in terms of humanism, rather than in terms of individualism.

Universalism meets the demands of the new age, because it is the product of those forces which created the new age. It does not send its roots down into a mediaeval civilization, interpreting past history. It does not come to the present weighted down with incrustations of traditionalism or of formalism, which inhibits spontaneous and contemporary action. Its theology expresses the modern conception of the nature of God and man. Its motive power arises out of the new humanism. Its axioms are the assumptions of the great social and psychical movements of the twentieth century. It is the real religion which the masses consciously or unconsciously are adopting. It is the philosophy and the power which under one name or another the multitudes are laying hold upon to swing this old earth nearer to the Kingdom of Heaven. It is the religion of the people, for the people, by the people. It is the faith of the new world life, sweeping upward toward spiritual expression.

A Free Church

A great historian has declared that organized religion has been the foe to intellectual, political and social progress. He has beheld, in the panorama of world events, the great institutionalized Church combatting the discoveries of science, tearing the prophet limb from limb and shackling the emancipator. But the historian fails to make the necessary distinction between the free and traditional forces of religion.

Churches have always been of two groups. The first contains those which have developed a vast and cumbersome organization which makes inertia almost inevitable. They have fulfilled the function of conservators of static racial, social and ethical ideals. They have acted as bulwarks of industrial and political systems. Their religion is a religion of authority; their theology is a theology of divine hierarchy; their organization stresses the value of ecclesiastical rites and ceremonies. The whole visible machinery and invisible atmosphere of such churches tends to create men whose thoughts are hedged about with law and custom, and whose spirits meekly recognize bounds. The typical product of such a church is completely satisfied with the *status quo*, and desires to spread the sanctions of ecclesiasticism about existent organizations, thus making them seem to be of transcendent origin. . . .

The other group of churches contains those fiercer, braver souls who passionately hunger after freedom of mind and soul, who are impatient of metes and bounds, and who are constantly endeavoring to push back the periphery of human experience closer to the universal and the divine. These are the freemen of religion, the pioneers of God. . . . A free religion is constantly endeavoring to surpass itself, to outgrow itself, to challenge the fundamentals of existence, to adapt itself to whatever new revelations may come with the dawn. . . .

The genius of Universalism is liberty. Its fathers dared to challenge the olden tyrannies of ecclesiastical authority, and interpret life in larger, more triumphant terms. Its beginnings are linked with stormy days of political and industrial revolution. Its prophets were stoned in the streets for their daring, they were ostracized by their contemporary complacent fellow religionists. But they fought the battles of religious and civil freedom, and today one of the most splendid characteristics of the Universalist Church is the unchallenged right of every individual to interpret the fundamentals of religion according to his conscience. . . .

Such intellectual liberation and broad fellowship, after winning the battle for theological freedom, have put Universalists in the forefront among defenders of the new science. They have been among the pioneers who have helped to harmonize science with religion. When it was heresy to believe in evolution, our fathers dared to proclaim it as a doctrine which would save religion, not destroy it, which would reveal God, not abolish Him.

But the fight for freedom is never won. Inherited liberty is not liberty but tradition. Each generation must win for itself the right to emancipate itself from its own tyrannies, which are ever unprecedented and peculiar. Therefore those who have been reared in freedom, bear a tremendous responsibility to the world to win an ever larger and more important liberty. . . .

The Universalist Church, though small in numbers, has ever been alive to the championing of social rights. In 1790 the Universalists put themselves on record against the holding of human beings as slaves. This is one of the first actions by a religious body in America. A slave was a charter member of the first Universalist Church in America.

One of the first and most effective champions of industrial freedom was Rev. Adin Ballou, author of "Christian Socialism" and founder of one of the first successful cooperative enterprises—that at Hopedale, Massachusetts.

The cause of women's liberation has been splendidly upheld. The first journal devoted to working women in this country was organized by a Universalist minister in the city of Lowell. The first national body of women organized in the United States were Universalists, and this denomination was the first to actively promote a woman minister. The second college in America to introduce coeducation was Lombard.

The cause of prison reform has been especially upheld by prophets of the larger faith before the science of penology was developed. The first great agitation against capital punishment, the first proposal of parole, and the first prison paper were instituted by Universalists.

They have been among the first agitators for Universal Peace in the modern world. The services of Clara Barton are famed throughout the world.

One of the first, if not the first resolution for total abstinence for individual and State, passed by a religious convention, was proposed by a body of Universalists, and one of the first temperance papers was run by a Universalist.

One of the first movements for the care and education of neglected children eventuated in the first Sunday school in America formed by Benjamin Rush, a Universalist.

Such has been the prophetic vision of Universalism. Such deeds it has contributed to the freedom of the world. The record of Universalism is emblazoned with mighty accomplishments. It has made bold the voices of clarion prophets; it has filled the eyes of humble men with imperishable visions; it has caused pulpits to thunder the larger good and the vaster hope; it has quickened the heart beat of the common life.

Such will be the untrammeled spirit of the new religion, and by such motive will the new church be inspired.

God and Democracy

All great social problems involve theological conceptions. We may divorce church from state, but we cannot separate the idea of God from the political life of the people. So intimate is the connection between religious and social development, that the history of tribal and national evolution reveals the fact that a particular type of theology is an almost inevitable concomitant of a particular type of society. There is a constant interaction between ideals of economic and political life on the one hand, and ideals of God on the other. As man attains increasing democracy, he conceives God as being more universal, more just and more intimately associated with life; and as God is conceived to be more universal, just and intimate, the idea begets more democracy among men. Social action and theological reaction are equal, and in the same direction. . . .

The old ideas of a God who created a spiritual aristocracy, who maintained partiality, whose sympathies were not as wide as the whole of humanity, are patently inadequate to meet the new needs. There is no mistaking the democratic instinct in the new man. He passions after freedom and brotherhood. He lays bare his heart and mind to the great human currents and exults in the tides of feeling which pour upon him, enriching and enlarging him. There is no mistaking the widening of sympathies, the greater sense of inclusiveness, the new solidarity of humanity. Such a humanity will no longer brook the imperious and fastidious God who has scorned the fellowship of most of his creatures in the past. A democratic people demand a democratic God, a robust deity who likes his universe, who hungers for fellowship, who is in and of and for the whole of life, whose sympathies are as broad as the "rounded catalog, divine, complete" . . . .

The Universalist idea of God is that of a universal, impartial, immanent spirit whose nature is love. It is the largest thought the world has ever known; it is the most revolutionary doctrine ever proclaimed; it is the most expansive hope ever dreamed. This is the God of the modern man, and the God who is in modern man. This is no tribal deity of ancient divisive civilization, this is no God of the nation or of a chosen people, but the democratic creator of the solid, indivisible world of rich and poor, black and white, good and bad, strong and weak, Jew and Gentile, bond and free; such a faith is as much a victory for the common people as was the passage of the Fourteenth Amendment to the Constitution. It carries with it a guarantee of spiritual liberties which are precedent to outward forms of governmental action. . . .

This poem was written in the early 1920s, after Skinner experienced a series of rebuffs and disappointments. He had been strongly attacked for his pacifism during the First World War and then for his liberal social views after the war was over. The poem appeared in Unity *on April 24, 1924.*

IN TIMES OF DISILLUSION

The world has grown unutterably old—
A place of bitter disillusionment.
Like some sad ruin out of ancient time
Half buried in obliterating sand,—
So seems the gallant world of yesteryear
To one who fellowshipped with wistful dreams.

Fair hopes did blossom for a flaming hour
And they were radiant. Bright youth went forth
In high imaginings, and all the world
Expectant and aglow, went forth with them
To greet the new age and new inbrothering.

But now the heart of the world is broken and sad,
The dream is spent—the curtains drawn—and those
Who strode to martial music, spoke great words
Befitting those great days, have laid aside
The mask of Jove-like visage and have shrunk
To lesser mould to play the cynic's part.
The candle that so mightily illumined
Has sputtered and gone out.
The house where we held rendezvous with hope
Is dark. The dream is gone. The dreamers go
In sad dismay to disillusionment.

Does God change masks when the curtain's drawn,
Put off high resolution and descend
To lower levels to play a lesser part?
Not God! That cannot be. No, God's not through.
There's hope immense to keep hope strong
And thrill the dreamer's soul with battle-call.
God's unsurrendered! He's God in that.
God's unsurrendered! So am I! For dreams
Outlast the dreamer. And when the great event
Is chronicled, 'tis vision will prove true—
The final truth in all events—supreme and ultimate.

Therefore I'll dream.
I'll light the candle yet again, illumine
The dark forsaken house, bring back the folk
Who thrilled at glimpses of a fairer world,
People the stage with pageantry and bid
Full panoplied illusion still enact

The epic of inbrothering.
I'll summon from out of time's unfathomed store
Great souls who, in the midst of hopeless days
Kept faith and knew the loneliness of God.
Those splendid deaths and yet more splendid lives
Which rallied their faltering age with valiantness
And left strong memories to breed strong hopes.
For such undying fellowship has power
To swell our shrunken souls to ampler mould,
And make us truer men.

I'll still proclaim the "Vision Splendid,"
'Till it strikes God-fire
In old and broken hearts, and urges on
The world to consummate its dream.
God's unsurrendered! SO AM I! Therefore
I will live communicate with hope. I light
The candle and—I DREAM.

Early in 1933, soon after he was appointed to the deanship of Crane Theological School, Skinner addressed the Universalist ministers in the Boston area, speculating on what challenges their ministry would face in the near future. A report of the meeting appeared in the Universalist Leader *for January 21, 1933, during the last days of the Hoover administration. Skinner's remarks were prefaced by the report's author.*

DEAN SKINNER TO UNIVERSALISTS

Some twenty-five ministers of the Universalist Church came through the storm January 9 to the regular session of the Boston Ministers' Meeting to hear Dean-elect Clarence R. Skinner of the Theological School of Tufts College on "The Universalist Church Twenty-five Years Hence."

The meeting was held in the Church of the Redemption. Dr. Huntley, president, and Mr. Raspe, secretary, were in their places. Dr. George E. Leighton of Somerville conducted the devotional exercises, assisted by Dr. Ulysses S. Milburn.

In the period of reporting on new books, Mr. Emmons recommended "Humanity's Great Need," by Hugh Woodward. Dr. Lowe spoke of "A Fortune to Share" and "Let's Start Over Again," by Vash Young. Dr. Milburn recommended "The March of Democracy," by James Truslow Adams, and "The American Note Books of Nathaniel Hawthorne," newly edited. Rev. Leslie Nichols recommended "Faith," in the January *Harpers.*

Dr. Huntley introduced Dean Skinner as a man of courage. Dean Skinner said in part:

Any one who attempts prophecy must be very courageous or very humble.

Technological change does not involve simply machinery. It involves thinking, living, working. It is natural for us who are brought up in certain ways of thinking to believe such ways can not change. Whoever looks back far enough in history will see how steadily changes come.

There will be two significant movements in the religious world in the next few years, and both of these movements will divide the Universalist Church. In fact there is no Universalist Church. There are Universalist churches. I do not believe it possible to unify the Universalist Church any more than it is possible to unify the Presbyterian Church.

One wing of the Universalist Church will become more conservative, in economic outlook, in social philosophy, in worship. And the more radical the social changes the more conservative these churches will become. I could pick out individual churches today and tell you which way they will go. Other Universalist churches, because of both laymen and ministers, because of lack of wealth, will drift toward the left sociologically and theologically. The great social problems are dividing people. The old unities are breaking up. Every one who has been an official in the Universalist fellowship must know these things to be true.

The great question is: Do the Universalist churches want to be socially creative, and help mold the standards of the future? Or do they want to hold on to the best of the past? Do we want to be molders of a future society quite different from society as we know it, and so be creators, or do we not? If we do, we must put ourselves in line with forces that are strange or hostile to the church as we have known it in the past.

The economic class movement, the labor movement, is working for a new order. If the Universalist Church wants to have a part in the future, it must get in line with these class movements.

I do not look for a Bolshevik communism to control in the United States, but I do look for a working class movement to transform society. The church that wants to be creative must get into it.

Science is making great strides. The nonscientific way of thinking is rapidly disappearing. A whole generation is coming into our colleges that has not spent one hour bothering with things outside the realm of fact. You must have observed this realistic trend. We have a generation that wants to know *what* more than it does *why* or *when*. It wants to base all programs on scientific analyses.

I am saying hard things. I am saying partial things. I know they are partial.

Young people are approaching problems not from the standpoint of what did Jesus say, or what does the Bible say, but from the standpoint of what does science say.

I think ministers can be too devoted to science. I believe religion has a basis other than that in science. But the scientific method must control our thinking if we are to serve in the new day. There again will not the Universalist Church split? Can the two wings hold together?

There is a new psychological approach and a new individualism. To see the best psychiatrists even now you have to make appointments two or three years in advance. People are not going to the church to find the solution of their problem unless the church employs the method of the psychologist. We are beholding a new generation, more honest, more free from false sexual ideals and ideas, more fearless.

Here again the church will split. Some will make the new approach to the individual. Some will not. We must make it if we are to remain liberal.

We must look forward to a time when the church will change so radically that preaching may disappear. The Christian Science Church has made the greatest progress in the past fifty years. It has no preaching.

There has got to be a profound change in the technique of church life, and specialized men will have to be developed for special departments.

I do not believe that preaching will disappear. I hope it will not. Fosdick preaches to ten million every Sunday. But consider how efficient Christian Science has been and how inefficient some of the rest of us have been, and face frankly this possibility of a new organization without preaching.

I want to ask you whether there is anything divine or sacrosanct about the kind of service we have. Do you realize that we have not made any real change in Universalist worship for one hundred years? Think about whether these forms that we use have any necessary validity. Can you not conceive of a service entirely different and vastly more efficient? I am coming to believe we can have a much more spiritual service without our old forms.

If the General Electric were presented with the problems confronting us, they would proceed in a scientific way. They would set aside men to try things out. Why can't we do that in the Universalist denomination? Why should all new things come down from above—from teachers or officials of the denomination? Why not have special churches acting as laboratories?

I'd like to see one Universalist church have the method of trying many men as preachers, putting in some other man as a parish worker. It might be tried in church like this. I'd like to see such a church made a liberal platform of preaching, the greatest men we can find employed, and see what happens. Would it be possible to experiment thoroughly with a Sunday evening forum? Scott in Peoria would be the type of man to try it. Try it for five years backed by the denomination, and publish the findings. I'd like to try an experiment in some beautiful church like this—have no preaching, but ritual, poetry, lights, colors, dramatics. This is, try the esthetic service.

It would be far sounder to put denominational money into some of these experiments than into keeping alive churches bound to go down soon anyway.

Then I'd try the experiment of making the church an educational center. Take the method of the Christian Scientist. Get a book. Try to put in a definite philosophy by a study method. Then after studying all the week come together as a class on Sunday with the minister as a leader. Publish all the results for the benefit of the rest of us. Possibly Melrose could put in a psychological clinic. Then I'd like to have our ablest men find out why such and such a man is so greatly beloved in his church.

Let all these things be reported on in five years, or ten years. Ministers then will have data to go on. They will know scientifically why this succeeds here and fails there. This will look forward to unification of weaker churches with stronger churches. The stress of time is crowding more churches to the wall. Others will fail. Perhaps if we planned we could put the churches together and employ two or three specialists.

I see dangers in the Free Church of America. I see

dangers in uniting churches and dangers in not uniting. The danger in not uniting is churches going on so feebly that they serve no useful purpose. The danger in union is that we may make a greater body of conservative opinion. That tendency may be seen in the Unitarian body today.

Early in 1939 the Crane Theological School faculty took turns presenting lectures on basic themes of religion, which were published as The Tufts Papers on Religion *in 1939. This is Dean Skinner's contribution.*

WHAT RELIGION MEANS TO ME

RELIGION. It is a word which inspires and confuses. It rouses passionate loyalties and equally passionate hatreds. There are those who see in it mankind sunk to its lowest depths of degradation. To some it is sublimely rational; to others it is stupid superstition. Theologians tell us that the world without religion would lose the highest values which keep man aspiring toward the best, and materialists tell us that without religion the world would be freed of the chains which bind it in slavery.

What is the meaning of this elusive, contradictory force which has wrought such strange results in the lives of individuals and in society? Are we able to experience it in this day and generation? Upon the answer hang momentous decisions, both for the present and for the future, for the individual and for society.

These questions are significant and important. They will not be lightly brushed aside, nor will indifference force them into complete silence. They are persistent problems for millions of people who attend services of religion, read about religion, discuss it, try to live it, and sincerely endeavor to wring from it the secrets which the great of old have found in it.

Ask ten people what religion is, and perhaps eight will reply uncertainly or will evade the questions altogether. Their answers, if attempted, are often intellectually muddled and emotionally embarrassed.

On the other hand, perhaps the answer will be so readily and glibly given that it betrays a mere cliché, an unthinking repetition of lifeless formulas. Ask these people what religion does for them and again they may be embarrassed, non-committal, evasive. Can they assert with conviction that because they have taken part in the services of religion they are in any concrete way different persons than they would have been if they had not participated in such services? Do their religious beliefs really matter?

What does religion mean to me? I answer that question in genuine humility.

Religion is something which exhibits infinite variety. It manifests itself under continually changing forms. I am content not to give it exclusive, narrow definition. As a wild bird prisoned in a cage will often refuse to sing, so the highest values, when dissected and confined within the bars of precise definition, will cease to function. Certain it is that the logician with his net cannot always capture art, love, personality, or religion. Just when he thinks he has them in his toils, they escape into the freer air of real life.

I am torn between forces: one making for intellectual clarity, the other making for depth and reality of experience. On the one hand, I do not want to lend myself to those who make for obscurantism by retreating into a welter of undirected emotionalism. On the other hand, I am inclined to believe that "in divinity and love what's best worth saying cannot be said." My answer to this dilemma is to be as clear and intelligent as possible about religion as it enters into my own life, but to be generous in allowance for differences in others.

Religion means to me the reverent attitude to whatever seems to the worshiper the greatest and best. It is not a mere subjective enthusiasm or glow of satisfaction, nor it is necessarily devotion to one objective reality whom we must call "God." It is both subjective and objective.

I feel something which is a profound and beautiful emotion. Frankly, gladly, I let that emotion become a part of my experience. I am not ashamed of it, or afraid of it, nor am I too greatly distressed if I cannot always define it or see all of its logical implications. It is closely allied to awe, love, worship, idealization, yearning.

My emotion is directed toward something. It has an object which is outside myself. That object is not always the same, nor do I always react in the same way to the same object. Under various conditions, at different times and in different moods, my greatest and best changes. But always it is something outside myself which calls to me, as I call upon it. Man is never without a something beyond himself toward which he aspires. In religion it is not the name of the object which counts most, but the active spiritual relationship between the soul of a man and that something. In religion it is not so much the achievement that is important as it is that man forever aspires, reaches and towers beyond himself.

I find great personal satisfaction in Whitehead's inspiring passage: "Religion is the vision of something which stands beyond, behind, and within the passing flux of immediate things; something which is real and yet waiting to be realized; something which is a remote possibility and yet the greatest of present facts; something that gives meaning to all that passes, and yet eludes apprehension; something whose possession is the final good, and yet is beyond all reach." ("Science and the Modern World.") It has been said repeatedly and insistently that religion is a way of life. It is that, but that statement does not differentiate religion from numerous other "ways of life." Agriculture, laboratory analysis and crime are ways of life, but they are not necessarily identified with religion. In the religious consciousness we find something more than morals, art, or social legislation. These are not excluded. They may be parts, but they are not the whole. Religion seizes upon almost any experience and lifts it into an ideal end which, as Dewey says, is pursued "against obstacles and in spite of threats of personal loss, because of conviction of its general and enduring value." ("A Common Faith.")

Some individuals may consider a hero or a loved one as the highest which imagination is capable of conceiving. If so, all the essential elements of religion are present in the experience: there are the emotional tensions of wistful yearning, the search for an object greater and better than himself.

We find this in Rama-krishna, a Hindu saint, as he knelt in single devotion and complete adoration of Mother Kali. Is not the reverent attitude of the Buddhist toward Gautama the essence of religion? For him the "Enlightened One" symbolizes the highest and holiest that he knows. Surely the undying loyalties of the devout Christian as he kneels before the figure of Christ are the very stuff of religious experience. Man-god or god-man has become a symbol of such high virtue and enduring worth that his personality expresses the greatest and best that some men can conceive.

Who does not feel the religious experience when he follows the career of Gandhi, when he reads of the beautiful life of St. Francis, or when he listens to the passionate appeal of Romain Rolland for a world of peace and internationalism?

Others may make religion of a group, such as a tribe or nation. It is hardly possible to read the lives of the great nationalists without realizing how close is their sense of devotion and sacrifice to that of religion. Limited their vision may be, but if the nation is the highest and best they know, their reverence before its symbols, their yearning for its glorification, contain all the elements of a religious experience. Marred by war as the history of nationalism has been, nevertheless it represents to millions the focus of their idealization and the expression of what is deepest in their lives.

To Joan of Arc, perhaps to a Hitler, nationalism may represent the will of God—the summation of ideal values for which they will gladly endure persecution and surrender their lives.

Some there are today who go beyond the confines of narrow race or warring state to bow before something far more majestic and awe-inspiring—humanity. The whole human race, past, present, and to come; not one divine person only, but all men and women, symbols of the highest. Scientists starving for truth, poets living in rags for love of supernal beauty, mothers clinging to their helpless brood, heroes dying in fire and flood, these are the greatest and best some men know. Comte, in the nineteenth century, worked out a religious service for the worship of humanity. Today many of the humanists declare that for them mankind stands at the end of their vista. It is the periphery of imagination: its struggles, defeats, hopes, and victories represent the holiest that we know. To get into the great stream of history, to sweat and sacrifice for truth, justice, and love—this is man at perihelion, this surely is religion enough.

Whosoever cannot be lifted unto heights by this

magnificent concept must be dull and unimaginative. Man's continual struggle for justice, his blazing wrath at wrong, his vision of a world of brotherhood—these are the very stuff of religion. They reveal man bowing before an ideal and utterly dedicating himself to it. The ideal enters into a man's inner nature, lifts it, broadens it, and fills it with undying flame.

There are some, however, who feel that they must go beyond even this inspiring vision. Their imaginations urge their search "to vaster issues," and the soul is restless until it has moved out to the uttermost boundaries of the universe. It will be satisfied with nothing less than the whole of reality. It feels kinship with atoms, persons, social movements, and galaxies of stars wheeling in silent majesty across infinitudes of space. This is the highest reach of the human intellect, this is the profoundest reality of the human soul, this is the greatest and best man can know. It is symbolized by the great word "God," but the word is not the reality. It is the experience that counts. Man is caught up into a sublimity that lifts him, liberates his deepest self, stretches his imagination, till it touches east and west, includes high and low, inspires and enriches him. This is the ultimate religion. In the great words of the poet Coleridge:

" 'Tis the sublime of man, his noon-tide majesty,
To know himself parts and proportions of one
wondrous whole."

To me the highest type of religious experience is

that which gives man a sense of unity and universality. Most of our life is spent in narrow segments. Our horizon is hemmed about by kitchen walls, office desks, narrow prejudices of race, class or creed. In religion, these partialisms, broken fragments of life, are lifted into a vast and profound oneness. Our littleness becomes stretched to cosmic greatness. Elemental forces roll through our beings, sensitize our perceiving, and quicken our lives. By a flash of insight we see in common things

The types and symbols of Eternity,
Of first, and last, and midst, and without end.

The spectroscope reveals the fact that man's body is made of the same elements as the farthest star. Chemistry proclaims man's kinship with the universe. Religious insight revealed centuries ago what physics and chemistry tardily proclaim. Man, from smallest cell to his total personality, is akin to the cosmos. We feel

Our destiny, our nature, and our home
Is with infinitude, and only these.

But one may say, men have stuck daggers into each other's hearts because they differed from each other as to the definition and description of this awful reality, or sublime being. As Lewis Browne graphically puts it in his description of Holy Jerusalem: "They have killed in this ancient town, killed until every alley was flooded with blood. Not a wall in all this maze of walls but has rung with the groans of the dying. Skulls beyond counting have been cracked on these flags; throats unnumbered have been slit in these dark doorways. They have murdered and pillaged and raped in this old holy town till now it is all but one Golgotha, one bloody hill of skulls . . . . And if you would know why, you need only look into the eyes of those hurrying phantoms. Readily they will tell you, explicitly. Men have slaughtered and ravished in Jerusalem, because they had—religion. Men have gouged eyes and ripped bellies because they—believed." ("This Believing World" . . . .)

This, however, does not invalidate the fact that religious experience has been and may be one of the profoundest and noblest experiences of the human race. A scalpel may be used to save a man's life or to destroy it. Chemistry may produce bread or bombs; this is no special problem of religion; it is a problem of human nature.

Religious emotions and enthusiasms may be made to serve either intolerant fear or the lovely life of peace and healing good will. The objective results of religion will depend upon the character and extent of our scientific knowledge, and the development of our philosophy, ethics, and sociology.

Central and imperative in the religious problem is the question, how is religion integrated into the rest of life? What part do reason, truth, and goodness play in this great experience which has been so universal? This question is what confounds so many, turning some to bitterness, and others to obscurantism.

Every aspect of life is inextricably bound to every other aspect. The individual and the social, the true and the beautiful, reason and emotion, are all facets of one reality. The interaction is inevitable. The best life is one that is integrated, a life which makes a consistent whole out of religion, science, art, ethics, the individual and the social. In this kind of unified life, science does not defy art or religion. Economics does not defy beauty or philosophy. Each makes its distinctive contributions to an harmonious whole. What is good for one must be good for all. What is true for one must be true for all.

Such a view saves religion from murderous fanaticism or ignorant superstition. It redeems from ugliness or individualism.

The problem of directing and integrating religion is no greater than the problem of directing and integrating science or economics. Science in the hands of selfish and brutal men can be prostituted to the ends of rapine and crime. Industrialism can be made to plunder and starve. Even beauty may be made to serve the ends of sensuous passion. The parts must serve the whole, and the whole must keep the parts functioning in relation to each other.

To me, religion (which in Latin means "I bind") is a force which lifts every individual and every aspect of culture into a unified whole. When one glimpses the meaning of the universal, the inner conflicts are resolved. Races, creeds, science and beauty are integrated into harmony. To me the possession of a universal point of view is the highest achievement of man. In it I find the solution of our most perplexing problems. As partial experience gives way to universal experience we find man growing in wisdom, dignity, and morality.

Let me close with the beautiful and pregnant words of Gilbert Murray:

"The Uncharted surrounds us on every side and we must needs have some relation towards it, a relation which will depend on the general discipline of a man's mind and the bias of his whole character. As far as knowledge and conscious reason will go, we should follow resolutely their austere guidance. When they cease, as cease they must, we must use as best we can those fainter powers of apprehension and surmise and sensitiveness by which, after all, most high truth has been reached as well as most high art and poetry; careful always really to seek for truth and not for our own emotional satisfaction, careful not to neglect the real needs of men and women through basing our life on dreams; and remembering, above all, to walk gently in a world where the lights are dim and the very stars wander." ("Five Stages of Greek Religion" . . . .)

Written during World War II, A Religion for Greatness *was published in 1945, the year of Skinner's retirement. Like* The Social Implications of Universalism, *published thirty years earlier, this book influenced the denomination heavily. A comparison between the two shows a significant shift in Skinner's conception of Universalism, from a liberal Christian position to one that might best be described as a global, mystical humanism. The concept of "the unities and the universals" is basic to* A Religion for Greatness. *Since the concept is complex and not fully developed here, the reader may find it useful to consider the universe, the economic system, and scientific knowledge as the* unities *and the body of basic values that might, in their application, move these unities toward the ideal as* universals.

A RELIGION FOR GREATNESS

RADICAL RELIGION

RELIGION TODAY faces a world not merely of transition, but of one revolutionary crisis following another with almost unbelievable rapidity. Political breakdown, economic paralysis, continental shifting of imperial power, stun the mind and spread disease. Hunger is so imperious that even a few hours may make men desperate. Our autonomic functions are not adjusted to the long view. The demands of the body are impatient and authentic.

In view of this fact, religion is in somewhat the position of the physician by the bedside of the despairing patient, or the social worker in a camp of hungry and bewildered refugees. A discourse on elemental realities seems to be so "far away and long ago" that it conveys no sense of relatedness to the actual. Undoubtedly religion, like medicine, social work and other institutional endeavors, must bend itself to the task of alleviating the suffering of the intensely now. It is not willing to stand idly by, doing nothing; yet it is ill suited to join in the debacle of hate and destruction. Yielding to the emergency, it is fitting that churches should be transformed into hospitals and Red Cross stations. Followers of different religious systems should shelter the homeless and keep up the morale of the victims of bombs.

Both religion and the world, however, are called to something more basic than the task of material alleviation and the binding of wounds. In view of the widespread tragedy of our day and generation, religion has a basic task to perform. It calls us to a searching of heart, a painful search which will perchance reveal us to ourselves as recreant to a great heritage. We are called upon to face anew elemental truths and to ask ourselves whether we have been wise and good stewards of these priceless treasures. We must go deeper than mere repetition of timeworn formulae. Our creeds and theologies, to which some of us have given our lives—are these shallow and empty? Are they without reality? Are they to be mercilessly cast aside as fossils of man's past illusions? Or is religion *the great reality*? Is it old but "old yet ever new," eternally reborn, capable of summoning a world to inward strength and dedication? Is religion still the sublime of man—the largest that he knows, the ultimate of his striving?

Perhaps we cannot give final answers to all these questions, but there is inspiration in the fact that the greatest religious leaders have refused to have their vision distorted by even the most appalling disasters of their time. They have insisted courageously upon upholding the deep and permanent realities of the spirit. The answer to the questionings of crisis was to go deeper into reality. [Skinner then cites examples from Confucius, Jesus, and Plato.] . . .

A final example will be given from the life of Augustine, who was certainly one of the greatest minds the church has ever produced, and one of the supreme influences in the Catholic medieval world for a period of over a thousand years. He lived in the period of despair when so-called barbarians were beginning to overrun Europe. Everything that was thought of as civilized was crumbling before the steady march of the hordes of the East. All the high achievements of Greek and Roman culture seemed suddenly to disappear. Art, philosophy, poetry, drama, that had taken five hundred years to produce, were snuffed out in a lifetime. Seemingly worst of all, Rome, the imperial city, was captured by Alaric, and with its fall the light of the world seemed to go out. Both Christian and pagan culture were threatened with complete extinction. Pessimism gripped the minds and souls of men and they began to give way to black despair.

In the midst of all this crisis, when every aspect of life seemed torn up by its roots, Augustine began to write his great theological treatise, *The City of God*. Certainly there must have been multitudes at that time who were unemployed, dazed, and starving, who wondered whether writing a book was the best contribution a great official of the church could make to such a period of crying need. There must have been great pressure upon the scholar to flee his library and go into the streets to comfort the dying and bring succor to the destitute. Very likely he did just that. But such charity, while needed, was not enough, so in 412 he began to write his greatest treatise and one of the great books of all time—*The City of God*. Not until 426 did he put the final words to this philosophy of history which was to give new life and hope to the people who sat in darkness. Fourteen years writing a book! And what years, when the very earth was shaking with the tramp of barbarian invaders and men's hearts were faint with fear!

That I call radical religion. The mind of this great seer, while not insensitive to the immediate and urgent problems of hunger and despair, set itself the arduous task of rethinking and reappraising religious fundamentals. Who can say that this elemental achievement was not more productive of good than if all the energy and vitality of this spiritual giant had been directed at ends less ultimate? He declared that the City of God was real, that there we can still find all the highest hopes and dearest dreams of man. The spiritual treasures of the ages still exist in the everlasting kingdom, and no Hun or Visigoth can destroy them. Such a faith kept candles flickering when all the other lights went out.

In this day and generation, likewise, when the highest achievements of the human spirit are in mortal peril of destruction, we dare say that a St. Augustine of the twentieth century will make a far greater and more lasting contribution to peace and justice than those who give themselves to immediate relief. What has radical-elemental-vital religion to say to broken and bleeding humanity? . . .

The Religion of the Unities and the Universals

[Prefaced by quotations from Chinese, Hindu, Christian, and Bahai sources, including this from Bahai: "That which is the cause of perfect unity and amity in the world of existence is the oneness of Reality."]

What, then, is this radical religion which goes down below surface appearance, and finds its root in the profoundest reality? How do we realize it in our lives? What have been some of its manifestations in history, and do we find that it has really been a common experience?

To sum the answer in a word, radical religion creates in man a sense of vital, meaningful relationship between the self and the universe. In primitive man this feeling may center in worship of sun, moon, stars, or other natural phenomena. It may manifest itself by the belief in and practice of mana—an all-pervasive potency which endows men with unique gifts. No matter how crude and superstitious man's early religion may have been, it lifted him out of his isolation into union with powers and influences greater than himself. His religious experience gave him an orientation toward the unities and the universals. Groping through fogs of ignorance he laid hold of the central fact of human existence; namely, that there is a relationship of dependence between man and the powers which exists outside and beyond himself.

Radical religion does not insist upon naming or describing these powers. Animism, polytheism, deism, theism, are phases of the essential experience, but none of these are necessary to it. The elemental fact is the outreach of man to something beyond himself. . . .

Three words will occur often in this essay; so often, in fact, that they may seem repetitious. To understand their meaning is vital to the understanding of the central theme of this essay. It will therefore be necessary to define these terms with as much precision as possible, and the reader is urged to fasten the definitions in his mind now, or to turn back to this page from time to time to refresh his memory.

The terms are of such a nature that they cannot be reduced to mathematical exactitude, but they are not so vague and discrete as to mean anything or nothing. They will be used with a certain connotation which is always in the mind of the author when he writes them.

Insight. The dictionary gives us the following: "A perception of the inner nature of a thing." In our view this ability may be purely intellectual, or it may be due to some causal factor which works in conjunction with intelligence. It may be close to intuition. Perhaps even some mystical quality may inhere in this ability to grasp the inner nature of some form of reality. Whatever the cause or character of the insight, we shall assume its validity when, like any other form of knowledge, we test it by empirical methods.

Unity. Again, the dictionary says, "The state of being indivisibly one; harmony, concord." This unity may be purely physical, as the unity of the human body; it may be intellectual, as the unity of a scheme or plan; it may be used as a metaphysical term, implying a fundamental unity underlying all aspects of reality. It may be used with all these meanings in this volume, but always it will mean the coherence of what may seem to be separate, into a oneness. Unity means an operative harmony, a functional relationship which belongs to all the parts of a whole.

Universal. Funk and Wagnalls says: "Relating to the entire universe; unlimited; general. Regarded as existing as a whole; entire. Including all of a logical class. A universal concept; that which may be predicated of many particular things or persons." We shall give all these connotations to the word. The universal will mean the all-inclusive as far as we can imagine it—the entire cosmos with all it contains. Again it will mean all of a class, as, a universal religion or a universal language. Finally, we shall mean by the term that which is the antithesis of the limited, or fragmentary. It is the opposite of the partial. When we speak of universalism we shall mean a philosophy of life or system of values which stresses the largest possible *Weltanschauung*, or world outlook, in contrast to the narrow view which is herein denominated partialism.

To return now to the consideration of the main theme of this chapter; namely, the fact that religion provides insight into these unities and universals. . . .

It is small wonder that we grow bitter at man's sinful partialisms. We have every reason to be rebellious against the stupidity and cruelty which turn the Elysian fields into a charnel house. But one fact persists through all our disillusioning and through all our attempts to make man naught but a miserable worm—a damnéd spot, to be erased and forgotten. That fact is the cosmic affinity of this same man, who in the most brilliant moments of flashing genius rises above the pettiness and indignity of his lesser self to the stature of the All.

Einstein, in his very brief essay entitled *Cosmic Religion*, says that there are three stages through which men pass in their religious development. First is the stage marked by fear of all the evils that beset mankind. A second and higher type evolves from the social feelings such as love and fellowship. Einstein believes that the anthropomorphic idea of God is common to these types, but there is a higher stage which he calls "cosmic religion." The individual feels "the nobility and marvelous order which are revealed in nature and in the world of thought. He *feels the individual destiny as an imprisonment and seeks to experience the totality of existence as a unity full of significance.*"

Here is a modern scientist, who certainly cannot be accused of sentimentality, recognizing just what we have been striving to express: man's existence and destiny as an individual (that is, as a separate unit) are a form of restriction and limitation. Separateness is an imprisonment. We find the meaning of human personality and the meaning of the whole universe in the unity of the parts with the whole. Just as a spark plug can be understood only when it is seen as part of an automobile, so man can be understood only when he is recognized as part of the universe.

Einstein tells us that "the religious geniuses of all times have been distinguished by this cosmic religious sense." Again, as we have been trying to say, the religious insight in its highest form perceives and conceives this quality of wholeness and inclusiveness, and believes it to be of the highest value.

Those who have experienced it in their personal lives have developed certain qualities which the world desperately needs. They have become "universe men" with an outlook so all-including that they can integrate into themselves all aspects of human, geographical, and even astronomical life. Examples of such personalities will be given in the next chapter. [Skinner's examples are Jesus, Peter, Paul, Albert Schweitzer, Walt Whitman, and Rabindranath Tagore.]

It is the further thesis of this essay that such personalities logically develop a social outlook which again is the basic and imperative need of our day. Because such men and women have experienced something cosmic and emancipatory, they inevitably reach out beyond the partialisms and fragments of human relations to those forms and practices of social life which are the largest and most inclusive. Both theoretically and practically the larger faith is creative of a social universalism.

To borrow a magnificent phrase from Herbert Agar: "It is a time for greatness." The crisis of our age which is one of the most acute in the whole history of man might well be described as a sudden demand for greatness for which the world is not prepared. Our trade, our civilization, have become unified and universal. As Wendell Willkie put it, there is "one world"—one physical neighborhood in which all the nations, races and classes have been thrown. But—and herein lies the crisis—we bring to this one world not a greatness and unity of spirit but a narrow provincialism. Our minds are filled with partialisms, while the physical forces of our culture are demanding and creating universalism. We cannot run a great society without greatness of spirit. We must have great conceptions, great imaginations, great emotions, great programs. We can't run a super-power dynamo with the steam from a teakettle.

There are two alternatives, and only two, before us. First, which is unlikely, is that we unscramble our modern interdependent culture, returning to separate and isolationist lives. If we went back to the village stage of existence, then we might be partialists to our hearts' content. Such a world would not *demand* greatness.

The other alternative is to so expand our spiritual powers that we vastly increase the range of our understanding and sympathy. There is no middle way. It is greatness—universalism—or perish.

There is no experience which gives to man so compelling a universalism as this radical religious insight into the unities and universals.

Economic Universalism

It is the contention of this essay that the religion of the unities and the universals should and does issue in various forms of social inclusiveness. We shall now proceed to discuss this contention in terms of economic life. . . . [In subsequent chapters Skinner discusses this contention in terms of race, politics, society, and science.]

To get down to the specifics and the modern application of our theory: what would this economic universalism be like in terms of today's culture? It would obviously mean building a system of production, distribution and consumption wherein the maximum number of human beings would be creative participators in the wealth of the world. What Bevan calls "the expansive attitude" which is distinctive of the religious personality would predominate over the contractive attitude which is characteristic of competitive business enterprise. The inclusiveness of the insight into the unities and the universals will demand that increasingly greater proportions of men and women shall be beneficiaries of our modern ability to produce. When we "see life steadily and see it whole" we cannot endure the concept of a world half poor and half rich. If we see the fundamental principle of the universe as a unity then we cannot tolerate a humanity divided into haves and have-nots. . . .

The problem of the [economic] revolution of the twentieth century is a complex one. We need a profound change not only in the system of production, distribution and consumption of material goods, but in the religio-ethical controls which should guide this change. Controls become obsolete, and idea-systems lose their ability to evoke loyalties. We can have well-meant revivals of the old dogmas, but they won't revive. The old fires are out. Shibboleths of the past simply do not rouse men's enthusiasm. Therefore we need a profound revolution, not only in the fundamentals of religion but in the whole system and terminology of its expression. No matter how painful it may be to outgrow the past, it must be done. Sentiments that are very near and dear to millions of hearts must be shattered rudely if their religion is to have reality and vitality enough to influence the development of modern society. Both science and philosophy seem to indicate clearly that the religion of the future will be in line with the cosmic consciousness. The unities and universals will triumph. . . .

The economic unities and universals of the future will naturally take a very different form from that of the primitive Christian community or from that of the medieval monastery. We have radically changed the techniques of production by our industrial revolution. We have evolved from farm and village life to the "great society." We have become mechanized, impersonalized, urbanized, cosmopolitanized. All this will profoundly affect the shape of things to come. The *agape* of the early Christians with its warm personal intimacy will be supplanted by something more formal and organized. Perhaps it will be implemented by governments, and be run as insurance, city planning, compulsory health measures, etc. Perhaps it will retain certain qualities of the voluntary system, as in our co-operative societies. Whatever it shall be, it must adapt the principles of responsibility for all men's welfare. It will recognize the solidarity of the human race and see to it that the terrible burden of poverty shall be lifted from the shoulders of all men.

It cannot endure a world half starving, half free. It must recognize the supreme fact of the unities and universals.

Scientific Universalism

Among the many challenging problems that must be met and solved in the near future is the relationship between religion and science. It is no mere academic question involving a handful of highly specialized thinkers whose interests are far removed from the common welfare. It is a question which is basic to the future world and it behooves all of us to do some hard thinking about it. It is a truly radical problem, for it goes to the root of our present maladjustment. . . .

These two great powers, religion and science should function with perfect harmony. They should be like the right and left hand, working together as one, carrying out a common purpose with a common integrated action. But one of the tragedies of civilization, both past and present, is the enmity which has existed between the two. Here we have the two greatest resources of the human spirit warring against each other! High purposes yearning to be embodied in reality, scorning the very process which could make their embodiment real. Systematic research and discovery of truth ignoring the ends which they are to serve. The result has been too often a religion obscurantist in its unwillingness to test its doctrines by the well-proven methods of investigation, and a science stubborn in its unwillingness to ask the fundamental question, what master it will serve. So we have a world tragically needing unity and the two forces most able to produce it divided and hostile. Until these powerful creative influences are brought into a functional harmony, the outlook for world civilization is indeed dark. If and when they can be integrated, working toward a common aim with a common method, what promise there may be for peace and brotherhood! . . .

The religion of greatness is big enough to believe in science *and* religion; in quantitative measurement *and* qualitative values; in exactitude *and* faith. It believes that any attempt to build satisfactory and lasting civilization on earth will fail unless these two great resources are brought together and made to serve a common purpose.

Can we do that, and if so, how?

The writer would suggest the following brief outline of procedure, which can be no more than suggestive, but at least marks the direction in which we must travel.

First, let both religionists and scientists cultivate a sense of humility, realizing that what we know is but a small fraction of what we do not know. . . .

Secondly, both groups must realize that both the methods of science and the methods of religion are complementary and each must be employed if we are to achieve a universal view. Very slowly the best minds in the various fields of science are coming to see that faith is as necessary in their work as in any other area of human endeavor. Think of the daring hypotheses which have been developed in astronomy, chemistry and medicine. It required creative imaginations of the noblest order to conceive the great changes which have taken place in these subjects. The men who dream dreams of emergent and revolutionary forces suddenly creating new heavens and new earths must be at least half poets, for no mere laboratory drudge could think such startling thoughts, or imagine such strange forms of reality. . . .

Finally, we must come to grips with one of the greatest problems of our time: Will science freely lend itself to any form which demands its service and pays its price? This is a hard problem—none harder—but perhaps the destiny of the human race depends on the answer. Science has put in the hands of man a power which makes him almost a god, and that power will grow in geometric ratio. Each new achievement will make dozens of new achievements possible, and so we will go on to a future of vast and profound implications. Perhaps we shall discover the method of releasing interatomic energy; or we may be able to create life in a test tube; perchance we can extract death-rays from interstellar space. Who dares say we can do none of these things and more? But if so, what of the human race? Shall we grovel in caves dug into the bowels of the earth and there become gradually extinct? Shall we draw every man, woman and child into a universal holocaust and there let them die in the horror of a future war?

These are not oratorical questions; they are real, pressing problems crying for solution. The answer can be found only when science tells us in unmistakable terms what it proposes to do. Can it continue to serve God and mammon? We believe not.

The great conflicts between science and religion today are along these lines. During the latter part of the nineteenth century the battle raged over theories of evolution, involving such issues as the inerrancy of the Bible, the origin of man and the materialistic hypothesis. These were challenging problems and men did well to bring to them their sharpest intellectual weapons. But such questions do not compare in magnitude with the issue which now confronts us. This is no academic theory. It may be life or death for mankind.

Let us repeat: The function of ethical religion is to reveal to man the great goals and purposes of life. Science is a method of solving problems. It is morally neutral. It can serve good or evil, democracy or autocracy, life or death.

Religion says: "The Lord our God is a jealous God. Him and only Him shalt thou serve." Science says: "I will serve God or the devil, Christ or anti-Christ, as it pleases me." There is the issue.

Science says to religion: "Your goodness is not wholly good if it be not true." Will religion have the courage to say to science: "Your truth is not wholly true if it be not good"? That is a bold question. It opens the floodgates of intellectual inquiry. It propounds fundamental questions regarding the nature of the universe.

The religion of greatness looks to the day when truth, goodness and beauty will become indivisible parts of the all-embracing unity and universal.

In May 1948 Skinner gave the keynote address at the annual meeting of the Massachusetts Universalist Convention. It was perhaps the last of his denominational acts, for he was terminally ill and died fifteen months later. In his valedictory, Skinner once again shared his vision of a world united by universal values, outlining ways in which it might be realized. The address was published in the Universalist Leader *of June 19, 1948.*

THE WORLD OF TOMORROW: WHO, WHAT, WHEN, HOW?

THE PRESENT MOMENT is the most exciting and challenging the world has ever known. The issues that are being fought out and wrought out are stupendous in significance and universal in scope. Nothing less than a world revolution is shaking the foundations of our lives; on its negative side, destroying much that we held sacred; on its positive side, building a new civilization.

The most important question that can be asked of any individual or group today is, "What is your attitude toward those creative forces which are girdling the earth?" The processes of history are forcing us to take sides. If ever the sheep and goats were parted, now is the time. It is the hour of decision when what we think and say and do, count. Neutrality is impossible for the issues of this revolution reach into the private life of every person and into every organized group.

The signs and portents are unmistakable for him who will look up and behold. It is as if a man were zooming across the sky in an airplane, writing in fire and smoke the word, "Revolution."

Prophecy is always precarious when the prophet indulges in specific detail, but it may be sound and true when announced in bold outlines. Today, we can blow the certain trumpet and declare with confidence there will be a new heaven and a new earth.

Who? The first question we must ask about the world of tomorrow is: Who are the people who will bring it in?

It may sound presumptuous to say that we can answer such a query, but I believe that we can. It will be the people who believe in the future, who have convictions about it, and who go forward, unafraid. . . .

Today, the spiritual heirs of the prophets, the men of vision, are to be the makers of the new earth. Those who cling to the past, who fear adventure, will go down with the past. Those whose courage fails them will try to beat a retreat and will run for some safe haven from the storm. But the hiding place will prove to be false. It will be blown down with the rest of the past. History is a one-way road. Once embarked upon it, there is no turning back. All the traffic surges forward, some swift, some slow, but it all moves forward. It is absolutely impossible to go back to Plato or Jesus, Thomas Aquinas or Karl Marx. We can learn from the past but we cannot go back to it. The only real true security lies in going onward, welcoming the new day waving Palm branches and singing glad Hosannahs in its praise.

What? The next question is what will the future be like? What kind of philosophy will dominate tomorrow's world? There is a bewildering variety of isms claiming to have the true solution of the world's problems: fascism, communism, capitalism, Unitarianism, pacifism, stateism, democracy, theism, Universalism. The followers of these philosophies believe that they are the true Messiahs whose sole function is to bring in the Kingdom of Tomorrow. Can we tell which has the truth? I think we can.

We must remember Walter Rauschenbusch's figure of the bird with one clipped wing. It always flies in circles, never being able to proceed to its goal. Only the bird with two whole wings can fly forward. This is a parable we will do well to remember. No one-eyed philosophy can meet all the needs of complex human beings. If we exclude from our minds all reality except one doctrinaire formula, we shall prove incompetent as guides and creators of the new world.

If we must contract the basic principles of tomorrow's civilization into a short formula, it will be that philosophy and plan of action which frees the *whole man* from the shackles of exploitation, ignorance, sin, superstition, provincialism, and enables him to live a fuller, more satisfying life. . . .

It is the deepest conviction of my life that it will come, this revolution,—sooner or later, peacefully or violently.

Does it mean Christianity? It ought to mean just that, for it was the founder of that religion who said: "I came that ye might have life and have it more abundantly."

But it does not mean the kind of Christianity we have had during the last hundred years. . . .

Does the future belong to communism? Perhaps. But communism to win the world must prove that it loves humanity more than power and that it is more interested to establish genuine justice for all than to serve its own exclusive terms of rule.

Whatever scheme of life wins out in the struggle to produce a new civilization must go *forward*. It must be bold in its conception, swift in action and above all, it must be *plural*. As Professor Sorokin says in his latest book, "The Reconstruction of Humanity," those who pin their hopes to one Messianic principle such as economical, spiritual, scientific or educational reform, will be disappointed. The future calls for a *whole* life for the *whole* man.

When? No language is too sensational to describe the urgency of the world's need. Shoes, clothes, medicines, coal, steel,—God knows we need these things desperately. But we need something more desperately, namely, a philosophy of life which will build a world in which man can live decently and peacefully with his fellow men. . . .

We cannot postpone the business of human destiny. Partisan politics, selfish indifference are sins if there ever were any. The world of tomorrow reaches out to us to save mankind from a repetition of the devastations of the past. *Now* is the day of decision. It *is* later than you think. We must hasten before we utterly lose our faith and creative power.

There is one thing certain; the longer we put off the world of the abundant life, the more violent the transition will be. . . .

How? Method is central to our problem. If we are to build a world of decency and sanity, we must take counsel as to *how* we shall accomplish that high purpose. The answer does not come from revelation. We must do some hard, realistic thinking and living if we are to discover the secret of effective method.

Sometimes, ends determine means. Sometimes means determines ends. Appropriate means make our objectives possible. Inappropriate means make our objectives impossible. We don't learn to play the piano by sawing wood and we don't build houses by setting forest fires. . . .

To try to solve problems by producing universal devastation merely produces despair which in turn produces more destructiveness. It is a vicious circle. How shall we break the circle and reverse the order?

By going *forward*! War with its pestilence is slavery to the past. It is an inheritance from barbarism which we should reject as we reject the inevitability of illiteracy or tuberculosis. Let us make a determined attack on this outworn method. Let us shake off the sense of futility which repeats the old adage, "It always has been, therefore, it always must be."

Let us lay aside the personal and national pride which insists on its own righteousness and which emphasizes the sins of all others who oppose us. Let us confess our own sins of omission and commission, pressing forward to new methods of living which are appropriate to the new world of tomorrow. One fraction of the effort put into building peace that is now put into building war would transform this old civilization into the Kingdom of Brotherhood. It would make possible the true revolution which the whole world eagerly awaits. Let us boldly determine to seek understanding, sacrifice, reconciliation, world organization.

Conclusion. We need spiritual giants in the earth who dare to break the shackles of the past; creative, onward-looking pioneers who dare to go forward.

We need a new philosophy which repudiates the old entrenched selfishness and exclusiveness of the past and which proclaims a more ample life for the growing spirit of man.

We must find new instruments of solving our problems; no longer the bludgeoning of the axe, but the effective methods of understanding and co-operation.

Above all, we must move forward NOW!

Forward! From Superstition to Reason; from Authoritarianism to Freedom; from Partialism to Universalism; from Individualism to Socialism; from Indifference to Conviction; from Fear to Faith; from Casualness to Discipline; from Anarchy to Organization; from War to Peace.

Skinner's final book consisted of three long essays and was apparently written when he was ill and near the end of his life. His close friend Alfred S. Cole edited the essays, and the book was published in 1955 by Kenneth Patton's Meeting House Press.

WORSHIP AND A WELL ORDERED LIFE

FROM BELIEF TO FAITH

IN THE PRESENT epochal struggle to objectively establish unity, justice, freedom and love, there is one quality which is primary. Without it there can be no better social order. The whole process of world rebuilding must begin with it, else our dreams of the golden age will be futile. That quality is pre-eminently religious; it is—faith. . . .

The author has had sufficient experience among the churches to know that whereas the average member loved to hear sermons and addresses on the new world order, if kept in vague and general terms, they were not ready to take the first step in making these visions real. They believed in most of the ideals as ideals, they loved the ideals, but not one in ten had faith that they were possible.

This paralysis of faith crept on unaware because we mistook faith for belief. But the two are not necessarily synonymous. Belief is an assent, frequently unreasoning and often passive. It is usually without the urge to creation. After the youthful era of courageous doubt has passed and we cease to challenge the established order, then we believe. After the schools have suppressed initiative and convention has lopped off aberrations from the dead line of conformity, then we believe. Belief frequently comes when we are tired of the fight, when our nerve is gone, and we are ready for a comfortable place in the chimney corner.

But not so with faith. It is an expression of unconfined zeal of spirit. It is for unsurrendered persons. Faith tries wings, follows illusions, challenges, urges, fails, conquers. It is more than the assurance of things not seen—*it is an adventure after them*. Belief digs itself into the trench of creed. Faith knows not horizons, can not live in crypts, behind padlocks. Faith is for eager and audacious persons. When belief takes the place of faith, creeds become paramount. When faith is dominant, deeds become the test. There is no issue between the old church and the new more clear than this: the old emphasized belief; the new must emphasize faith. . . .

Can there not be a social and political mysticism which calls forth an eager faith? Can we not visualize a better world which is not yet real, but which is capable of becoming a reality? And why does not religion furnish us a faith in the possibility of that world? This sort of mysticism would call for high powers of divining, a sharp spiritual insight, and more, it would call forth creative ability. . . .

The partial religious life of the past failed to give us this spirit because it overemphasized the value of submissive belief and underemphasized the infinitely more important virtue of creative faith. The function of the church in the reconstruction of society must be the fostering and enkindling of this new spirit. The world cannot live on mere attitudes and gestures and assents. To reach an intellectual or spiritual stereotyped form is a death warrant to progress. The new task is to incite to upward and outward movements; it is to urge action; it is to achieve.

Never was there a time which called so insistently for so prodigious a faith as at present. . . .

What Is Worship?

Worship exists wherever there is a tension between the individual and an object which he reverently holds to be of highest significance and value. It is the outreach of man to attain union with this object—to know it, to feel it, to experience it. . . .

Dr. Meland asks, "Can this generation worship?" The answer is, we can do no other. We may not be able to worship the same objects as in the past, or to express our need in the traditional forms; but man is so made that he simply cannot escape the necessity of reaching upward and outward toward something greater than himself. That something may be an unachieved ideal that beckons and urges him; it may be the summation of the sustaining forces of the universe; or, sad to say, it may be a brutal social order which exalts naked power. Whatever the unseen and distant goal, man never has lived a dreamless life, content to adjust his whole being to things as they are. The light that shines for him "never was on sea or land." For the vision splendid he will set in motion a million-footed army, he will fly in the air, and penetrate the infested swamps. Nothing seen or known can satisfy the hunger of our hearts and minds. In the dust that is man there shines an unearthly flame.

A Well Ordered Life

Dear Lord and Father of Mankind!
Forgive our foolish ways!
Reclothe us in our rightful mind,
In purer lives thy service find,
In deeper reverence praise.

Drop thy still dews of quietness,
Till all our strivings cease;
Take from our souls the strain and stress
And let our ordered lives confess
The beauty of thy peace.

These words of John Greenleaf Whittier strike a universal note. We know what it means to crave release from strain. Confusion distracts our minds and burdens our shoulders. The cruelties of war leave us with psychological wounds which may never wholly heal. Anxieties invade the sanctuaries of the inner life with harsh insistence. Strain within and turmoil without—how can we meet them with quiet dignity? There must be a way or ways.

Philosophers and religious leaders have believed that underneath the surface storms of life it is possible to find "the deeper life of unshaken composure." As the fiercest hurricane cannot reach to the ocean depths, so the most violent disturbances do not necessarily reach the area of calm and poise which is at the center of a strong personality. A quiet dignity is native to the soul. Children often possess it, and so-called savages frequently manifest it. If we let misfortune rob us of an ordered life, it is largely our own fault, due to our attitude toward the misfortune. It is possible to face shattering experience without being shattered, and it is possible to go to pieces because of the most trivial experience.

There are men who have known a full measure of human suffering and yet remained unswerved and unsurrendered. There are others who crumble under the slightest blow; because of an unhappy experience they let their lives disintegrate. The difference between being broken and living a spiritually well ordered life cannot be explained in terms of what happens to us.

Things and events do not break us. We go to pieces because we bring to life a breakable philosophy. If we bring to crises a habitual attitude of quiet thinking and unfrightened adequacy, we can meet the most devastating experiences and still maintain our integrity. . . .

A well ordered life is that quality of character which enables a person to face outward disorder with a sense of calm, meeting the threat of disorganizing forces with an assurance of power equal to the danger. He is determined to live, not according to outward circumstance, but according to his own integrity.

An ordered life means purpose rather than drift. A weak man yields to temptation because he has no inner direction. With him necessity is greater than purpose. In a well ordered life, *purpose is a necessity*.

Finally, a life is ordered or disordered depending upon whether it has an authoritative value or categorical imperative as its organizing power. I shall not speak of "eternal values," for we cannot say what passes beyond time. But we can speak with confidence of time-tested values which experience declares to be basic to spiritual health. Justice and righteousness, beauty and truth, mercy and love: these are the foundation of all order. They create order and spiritual health among those who base their lives upon them. All spiritual regimen begins and ends with them. When we recognize such ideals as having enduring worth, and when we have creative faith in them, we cannot splinter into fragments at the first onslaught of destructive experience.

AFTERWORD

FOR SEVERAL DECADES after his death, the name, memories, and ideas of Clarence Skinner were kept alive by those who had known him firsthand, primarily the students he taught and his colleagues at the Crane Theological School. Among those students were Gordon McKeeman, Albert Ziegler, Earle McKinney, David Cole, Raymond Hopkins, and Keith Munson, all of whom rose to positions of denominational leadership. In 1955 Skinner's colleague Alfred S. Cole helped to get *Worship and a Well Ordered Life* published, and three years later the Social Action Committee of the Massachusetts Universalist Convention established the "Clarence R. Skinner Award," to be given annually to the preacher of the sermon that "best expressed Universalism's social principles." The Unitarian Universalist Association continued this yearly tradition after the two denominations consolidated. In the 1960s the *Annual Journal of the Universalist Historical Society* devoted considerable space to Skinner's contributions; the journal even reprinted *The Social Implications of Universalism*. James Hunt of the Crane faculty served as editor for much of Skinner's work during this period. Soon after the consolidation of the American Unitarian Association and the Universalist Church of America in 1961, the newly created Unitarian Universalist Association purchased a building and named it *Skinner House*, and *Skinner House Books* became the publishing imprint for denominational publications designed primarily for Unitarian Universalist readership.

During the first few decades of the merged denomination, its Universalist component, including Skinner's contributions, was largely overshadowed by the Unitarian segment, in spite of the UUA leadership's best efforts and the publication of several important Universalist texts. These included Ernest Cassara's *Universalism in America: A Documentary History in 1971*; George Huntston Williams' *American Universalism: A Bicentennial Historical Essay* as Volume IX of *The Annual Journal of the Universalist Historical Society* in 1971 (republished in 1976 by Beacon Press); and Russell Miller's two-volume history, *The Larger Hope*, in 1979 and 1985.

Beginning around 1980, however, a renewed interest in Universalism and its history began to emerge, and through seminary classes, lectures, convocations, and the printed word, the contributions of Clarence Skinner became familiar to a new generation of Unitarian Universalists. It has become increasingly apparent that Skinner was largely responsible for the work of creating "a new Universalism," with a fresh approach to theology and a renewed commitment to social responsibility, in the years just before World War I with publication of *The Social Implications of Universalism*. He continued this work throughout the rest of his life, writing *A Religion for Greatness* during World War II and clearly calling for fundamental changes in Universalist theology and practices. Following Skinner's death the work was carried forward, not only by his students and colleagues but also by such men and women as Dorothy Spoerl, Angus MacLean, Robert Cummins, Clinton Scott, Philip Giles, and Kenneth Patton. Indeed, the work continues today.

ACKNOWLEDGMENTS

The help of the staff of Skinner House Books and its editorial board is acknowledged with deep appreciation, particularly that of its publications director, Patricia Frevert, and its editor, Mary Benard. I also wish to express my indebtedness to Charles Gaines, James D. Hunt, Alan Seaburg, and the late Carl Seaburg, all of whom made major contributions to an earlier book, *Clarence R. Skinner: Prophet of a New Universalism*, published by Skinner House Books in 1999 but now out of print, on which much of the present volume has been based.

—C. H.